بسم الله الرحمن الرحيم

"The house of al-Arqam is the house of Islām"

Al-Ḥākim (d.405 h) in *al-Mustadrak ʿala al-Ṣaḥiḥayn* (6185)

THE NECESSITY *of* ḤADĪTH

And the Disconnect between the Qur'ān-only Approach and the Qur'ānic Text

Farīd al-Baḥrainī

DAR AL-ARQAM

ISBN: 978-1-8384897-4-8

British Library Cataloguing in Publishing Data
A catalogue record for this book is available from the British Library

Prepared and published by Dar al-Arqam Publishing,
Birmingham, United Kingdom

Authored by:

Farid al-Bahraini
He is a published author and editor of Islamic books in the Arabic Language.

www.daral-arqam.co.uk
Email: daralarqam@hotmail.co.uk

The Necessity of *Ḥadīth*

And the Disconnect between the Qur'ān-only Approach and the Qur'ānic Text

Farīd al-Baḥraini

الفهرس

Contents

Preface

In the name of Allah the Most Gracious Most Merciful.

The *ḥadīth*-rejection movement isn't organized. It doesn't have an *imām*, a body of scholars, or a governing body. It is a reaction.

A decade ago, I recall sitting on indoor steps that led to a roof, facing two acquaintances, when a *ḥadīth* was brought up. One of them objected saying, "But how do we know that the *ḥadīth* got to al-Bukhari correctly?" or something along those lines. The other smiled, clasping the hand of his partner, upon discovering that they shared the same line of thinking.

I did not hesitate to explain the *ḥadīth* system succinctly as they sat silently, smirks now gone, dumbfounded by the new information. It was clear that they did not know about *ḥadīth* sciences, but what struck me was that they were conservative Sunnī laymen, not militant Qur'ānist types.

What exactly would lead to this stance, this skepticism, towards *ḥadīth*? What would cause a Muslim to reject the teachings of the prophet that he adores?! It is a reaction to narrations that appear to be problematic.

Yes, those same narrations that are brought up by critics of Islam, heretics, and opposing sects; the same ones that have been debunked on all mediums throughout the centuries. Unlike the traditional

Sunnī that stands his ground, those affected by "Qur'ānism" turn their backs on the *ḥadīths*, dismissing them as non-authoritative. However, this position, which may appeal to some in the short run, undermines Islam as a whole.

It is with the above in mind that I've decided to write these pages, to demonstrate to the reader, the misguidance of the Qur'ānists and the necessity of *ḥadīth*.

Farid al-Bahraini

Introduction – The Need for *Ḥadīth*

Imagine a religion in which its adherents openly reject every saying, action, and event surrounding their prophet.

It is a Qur'ānist's reality.

The inability to come to terms with certain aspects of Islam has led the Qur'ānist to the complete rejection of the *ḥadīth* corpus. Often, these reports conflict with their modern secular liberal values that are irreconcilable with some of what can be found within the *ḥadīth* literature. This extreme stance bears multiple predicaments, some of which are clearer than others.

The most obvious of these pertain to the obligation of observing prayers and paying of the alms. The details of these Qur'ānic orders are expounded upon in the *ḥadīth* literature. However, that is just the tip of the iceberg.

Everything about Islam is questionable without *ḥadīths*. What exactly do we know about the Prophet of Islam ﷺ without *ḥadīths*? Nevermind his biography, we can't even ascertain his identity. The Qur'ān only identifies him as Muḥammad (Q. 3:144). Couldn't this be referring to Muḥammad bin Maslama (d. 43 AH) instead of Muḥammad bin 'Abdillāh (d. 11 AH)?

The rejection of *ḥadīth* widens the increasing gap between us and the Qur'ān itself. External matters like the compilation of the Qur'ān, our access to the Qur'ān through recitation, and our understanding of the Qur'ān, are all deeply rooted in *ḥadīth*.

Yes, the root of the problem, when it comes to *ḥadīth* rejection, lies in the Qur'ānist's perception of certain *ḥadīths*. Ideally, the Qur'ānist should be approached with the answers to their queries which caused the doubts in the first place. However, this manner of tackling the problem isn't efficient due to the diversity and volume of arguments; besides, answers to the vast majority of doubts are easily accessible across the internet. Hence, the aim of this work is to demonstrate the necessity of *ḥadīth*, for that alone should cause the Qur'ānist to doubt the validity of their position.

The First Generation of Muslims

The Ṣaḥābah and the *Ḥadīths*

Discussions with Qur'ānists revolving around the obligation to follow *ḥadīths*, or its impermissibility, often begin with the quoting of Qur'ānic verses.

Adherents to *ḥadīth* will often quote verses like:

يَا أَيُّهَا الَّذِينَ آمَنُوا أَطِيعُوا اللَّهَ وَأَطِيعُوا الرَّسُولَ وَأُولِي الْأَمْرِ مِنكُمْ ۖ فَإِن تَنَازَعْتُمْ فِي شَيْءٍ فَرُدُّوهُ إِلَى اللَّهِ وَالرَّسُولِ إِن كُنتُمْ تُؤْمِنُونَ بِاللَّهِ وَالْيَوْمِ الْآخِرِ ۚ ﴿٥٩﴾

> O' you who have believed, obey Allah and obey the Messenger and those in authority among you. And if you disagree over anything, refer it to Allah and the Messenger, if you should believe in Allah and the Last Day. (Q. 4:59)[1]

---

1 The usage of this verse as evidence for the adherence to ḥadīth is based on the differentiation between the obedience of Allah the Almighty and the Messenger ﷺ. "Obeying the Messenger" cannot be interpreted to mean "obey the Qur'ān" or "obey the message of Allah." Had that been the case, the word "messenger" wouldn't have been used. Some Qur'ānists might object that we do not have physical access to the Messenger ﷺ, hence, we cannot obey him. However, the same can be said about Allah the Almighty. Ultimately, we have His book, and we obey Him through His book. The same applies to the Messenger ﷺ, whom we obey through his narrations.

The Qur'ānist, on the other hand, would quote verses like:

Do they not look into the realm of the heavens and the earth and everything that Allah has created and [think] that perhaps their appointed time has come near?

فَبِأَيِّ حَدِيثٍ بَعْدَهُۥ يُؤْمِنُونَ ﴿١٨٥﴾

So in what ḥadīth hereafter will they believe? (Q. 7:185)

Such discussions may be, at times, fruitful, but often don't lead to results for an obvious reason. The discourse surrounding the authoritativeness of the *ḥadīth* did not exist during the revelation of the Qur'ān. Hence, there are no clear-cut verses that state anything like, "Follow the non-Qur'ānic teachings of the Messenger," or "those who seek the Messenger's teachings outside the Qur'ān are misguided." What we can be sure of is that the first generation of Muslims had a clear idea of the correct position to take, despite the lack of existing verses of this nature.

And what was the position of the Companions of the Prophet ﷺ in regards to *ḥadīth*? Obviously, they adhered to them.

Of course, the skeptical Qur'ānist isn't going to take our word for it, so a few more questions are required to determine what prevents them from accepting this well-established fact.

It is important to remind the Qur'ānist that the discussion doesn't revolve around the authenticity of a *ḥadīth* itself. Often, a Qur'ānist will raise the bar of required evidence for authenticity to an unreasonably high level in order to reject narrations. They claim: "One should not be lenient when it comes to the religion." However, this discussion is not about the implementation of a religious ruling, it is merely an inquiry regarding the adherence to *ḥadīth* by historical personalities. In other words, it isn't about whether the Prophet ﷺ did something, but rather, it is about whether a historical personality believed he did.

Does the Qur'ānist accept the **existence** of prophetic narrations in classical compilations?

Anything apart from an affirmative answer should abruptly end the conversation since the other party cannot be genuine if they deny the existence of reports in classical compilations.

Moving on...

Does the Qur'ānist accept the attribution of classical works to their authors, for example, the *Muwaṭṭa'* of Imām Mālik (d. 179 AH)?

The question is significant because it establishes an early date for the circulation of *ḥadīths*. Some Qur'ānists may be of the opinion that all the *ḥadīths* in our possession are third century attributions, if not further. However, if Mālik did indeed pen the *Muwaṭṭa'*, then the circulation of *ḥadīths* must have occurred during the first three generations of Islam.

A fair Qur'ānist would not assume that the *Muwaṭṭa'* is a false attribution, but in case we are dealing with an unreasonable Qur'ānist, we would need to make them aware that the scholars of *ḥadīth* have listed over sixty students of Mālik that narrated his *Muwaṭṭa'*.[2] Several of these were preserved in manuscript form, printed, and made available to us, like the *riwāya* of al-Shaybānī (d. 189 AH), al-Qa-

2 Al-Yaḥṣubī, *Tartīb al-Madārik*, 1/199-202.

ʿnabī (d. 221 AH), al-Laythī (d. 234 AH), Suwayd bin Saʿīd (d. 240 AH), and Abū Muṣʿab (d. 248 AH). The *Muwaṭṭā* was circulated by those students from Persia to Andalusia.

Once this is established, the Qurʾānist needs to be aware that Mālik was actually born in the year 93 AH. Due to this, a rather large number of his reports, 153 in total, include only a single narrator between him and the Companion. *Thunāʾiyāt Muwaṭṭā Mālik* by al-Fayḍī is a useful resource for these narrations. Mālik narrates these reports from his following teachers: Nāfiʿ, Isḥāq bin ʿAbdillāh bin Abī Ṭalḥah, ʿAbdullāh bin Dīnār, al-Zuhrī, Abū Ḥāzim Salamah bin Dīnār, Sharīk bin ʿAbdillāh bin Abī Namir, ʿAbdullāh bin ʿAbdillāh bin Jābir bin ʿAtīk, al-ʿAlāʾ bin ʿAbd al-Raḥmān, Ḥumayd al-Ṭawīl, Muḥammad bin Abī Bakr al-Thaqafī, Abū al-Zubayr al-Makkī, Muḥammad bin al-Munkadir, ʿAmr the *mawlā* of al-Muṭṭalib, Nuʿaym bin ʿAbdillāh al-Mujmir, Zayd bin Aslam, Rabīʿah bin ʿAbd al-Raḥmān, Saʿīd al-Maqburī, Wahb bin Kaysān, and Yaḥyā bin Saʿīd.[3]

The Qurʾānist will naturally ask: "But why trust Mālik in the first place? Isn't it possible that these reports were fabricated by him?"

The Qurʾānist should be glad to know that they are not alone in their skepticism towards the narrators of *ḥadīth*. Even a major narrator like Mālik was scrutinized. However, as opposed to the modern Qurʾānist, the scholars of *ḥadīth* placed the narrators into categories, weak and strong, instead of dismissing all reports altogether. Skepticism led to filtration, not indiscriminate rejection, and one of the ways in which they would judge the narrator is by examining their

3 Al-Fayḍī, *Thunāʾiyāt Muwaṭṭā Mālik*, p. 67-70, 72, 75, 77-78, 81, 85, 93, 107-109, 112, 116, 135.

reports in order to find corroborations.

For example, the very first report in the book is from Nāfiʿ (d. 117 AH) narrating from Ibn ʿUmar that the Prophet ﷺ said, "If someone misses the *ʿaṣr* prayer it is as if he has suffered a great misfortune in his family and wealth."[4] The same report can be found narrated by Ṣakhr bin Juwayrīyyah,[5] al-Ḥajjāj bin Artȧa,[6] Ayyūb al-Sakhtiyānī,[7] and al-Layth,[8] all from Nāfiʿ.

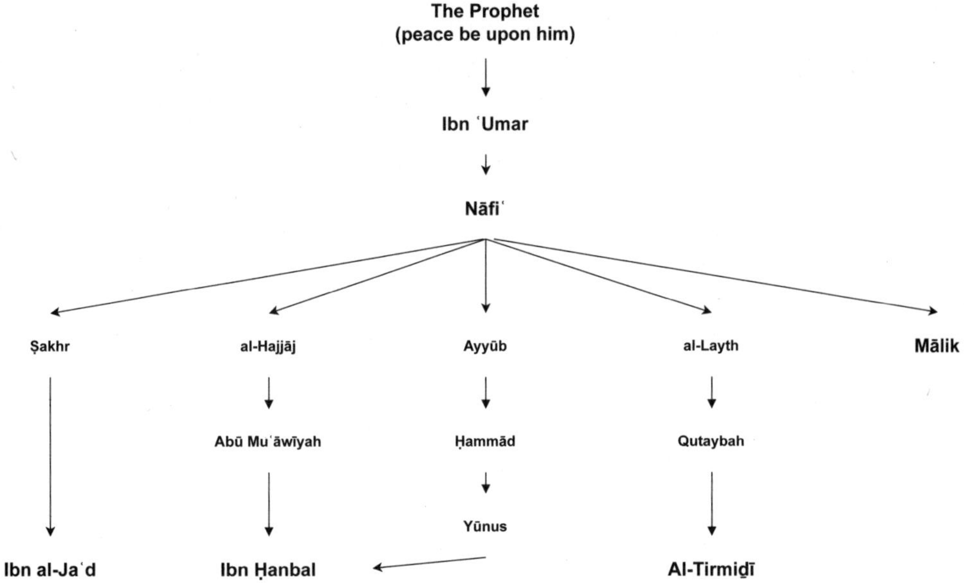

4 Ibid., p. 67.
5 Ibn al-Jaʿd, *Musnad Ibn al-Jaʿd*, p. 442.
6 Ibn Ḥanbal, *Musnad Aḥmad*, p. 343.
7 Ibid., p. 425.
8 Al-Tirmiḏī, *al-Jāmiʿ al-Kabīr,* p, 84.

The above image refutes the assumption that the report was concocted by Mālik. Thus, the Qur'ānist that insists that this report is a fabrication is limited to two scenarios. Either this report was concocted by Ibn 'Umar or his student Nāfi'. Fortunately, multiple classical sources attribute the same narration to Ibn 'Umar's son, Sālim,[9] so while it is certainly still a possibility that both Sālim and Nāfi' colluded in concocting this report, it is much likelier that this narration was uttered by Ibn 'Umar himself.

The second report in the book[10] is also narrated from Mālik's teacher Nāfi' through Ayyūb, his other student.[11] The third report in the book[12] is supported by two other narrators from Anas, the companion that is narrating the *ḥadīth*. In other words, three students of his are narrating the same *ḥadīth*.[13] In other words, there is no difficulty in tracing these narrations to the first and second generations of Muslims.

Narrating *ḥadīths* was very common from the very first generation of Islam. Ibn Ḥazm lists 1018 narrators from among the Companions. The first four caliphs also fall within the top thirty narrators.[14] The most prominent of these Companions have a lengthy list of students, whose names were compiled alphabetically within their bi-

---

9 Al-Ṭayālisī, *Musnad Abī Dāwūd al-Ṭayālisī*, p. 336; Ibn 'Asākir, *Tārīkh Dimashq*, 28/638.

10 Al-Fayḍī, *Thunā'iyāt Muwaṭṭā Mālik*, p. 67.

11 Ibn Ḥanbal, *Musnad Aḥmad*, p. 335.

12 Al-Fayḍī, *Thunā'iyāt Muwaṭṭā Mālik*, p. 68.

13 Al-Nīsāpūrī, *Ṣaḥīḥ Muslim*, pp. 1064-1065.

14 Ibn Ḥazm, *Asmā' al-Ṣaḥāba al-Ruwāt*, pp. 44, 56-57.

ographies: Abū Hurayra with 310 students,[15] Ibn ʿUmar had 236,[16] Anas taught 223,[17] ʿĀʾishah narrated to 210,[18] and 194 heard from Ibn ʿAbbās.[19] Any suggestion entailing the idea that these companions were Qurʾān-only or that none of these students ever heard from them would require substantial proof.

To reiterate, when determining the origins of these reports, it is unreasonable to claim that narrations are late fabrications by the compilers, for we find thousands of common links that push for an early dating of the reports. Unless one were to unreasonably claim that all of these narrations were fabricated in the second generation, it is safe to say that much of what has been narrated truly came from the Companions of the Prophet ﷺ.

Types of Narrations by the Companions

Some Qurʾānists, due to the diverse nature of the movement, may be softer with narrations than others and may argue that the Companions of the Prophet ﷺ did narrate *ḥadīths*, however, these *ḥadīths* had nothing to do with rulings. In other words, in order to reconcile their opinion that the Qurʾān condemns *ḥadīths* with the fact that the Companions narrated *ḥadīths*, they'll conclude that prophetic *ḥadīths* don't include religious rulings.

This reconciliation, while creative, conflicts with Qurʾānic verses, and *ḥadīths* of course, that allude to non-Qurʾānic rulings.

15 Al-Mizzī, *Tahḏīb al-Kamāl*, 34/367-377.
16 Ibid., 15/334-338.
17 Ibid., 3/354-363.
18 Ibid., 35/228-233.
19 Ibid., 15/156-161.

One of these verses speaks of intercourse during Ramadan:

أُحِلَّ لَكُمْ لَيْلَةَ الصِّيَامِ الرَّفَثُ إِلَىٰ نِسَائِكُمْ ۚ هُنَّ لِبَاسٌ لَّكُمْ وَأَنتُمْ لِبَاسٌ
لَّهُنَّ ۗ عَلِمَ اللَّهُ أَنَّكُمْ كُنتُمْ تَخْتَانُونَ أَنفُسَكُمْ فَتَابَ عَلَيْكُمْ وَعَفَا عَنكُمْ ۖ
فَالْآنَ بَاشِرُوهُنَّ وَابْتَغُوا مَا كَتَبَ اللَّهُ لَكُمْ ۚ وَكُلُوا وَاشْرَبُوا حَتَّىٰ يَتَبَيَّنَ
لَكُمُ الْخَيْطُ الْأَبْيَضُ مِنَ الْخَيْطِ الْأَسْوَدِ مِنَ الْفَجْرِ ۖ ثُمَّ أَتِمُّوا الصِّيَامَ إِلَى
اللَّيْلِ ۚ وَلَا تُبَاشِرُوهُنَّ وَأَنتُمْ عَاكِفُونَ فِي الْمَسَاجِدِ ۗ تِلْكَ حُدُودُ اللَّهِ فَلَا
تَقْرَبُوهَا ۗ كَذَٰلِكَ يُبَيِّنُ اللَّهُ آيَاتِهِ لِلنَّاسِ لَعَلَّهُمْ يَتَّقُونَ ﴿١٨٧﴾

> **You are permitted to lie with your wives during the night of the fast: they are as garments to you, as you are to them. God was aware that you were betraying yourselves, so He turned to you in mercy and pardoned you: <u>now you can lie with them</u>- seek what God has ordained for you**- eat and drink until the white thread of dawn becomes distinct from the black. Then fast until nightfall. Do not lie with them during the nights of your devotional retreat in the mosques: these are the bounds set by God, so do not go near them. In this way God makes His messages clear to people, that they may guard themselves against doing wrong. (Q. 2:187)

The verse indicates the existence of a ruling that cannot be found within the Qur'ān, pointing to the prohibition of intercourse during Ramadan nights. Ibn 'Abbās explains that initially "during the lifetime of the Prophet ﷺ, when the people offered night prayer, food, drink, and women, became impermissible to them, and they kept fast till the next night."[20] This ruling that is expounded upon in the report, is alluded to in the verse, and cannot be found in the Qur'ān. It is a clear proof of a non-Qur'ānic revelation about a prohibition.

Another example of non-Qur'ānic revelations can be found in verses that speak of the direction of prayer.

سَيَقُولُ السُّفَهَاءُ مِنَ النَّاسِ مَا وَلَّاهُمْ عَن قِبْلَتِهِمُ الَّتِي كَانُوا عَلَيْهَا ۚ قُل لِّلَّهِ الْمَشْرِقُ وَالْمَغْرِبُ ۚ يَهْدِي مَن يَشَاءُ إِلَىٰ صِرَاطٍ مُّسْتَقِيمٍ ﴿١٤٢﴾ وَكَذَٰلِكَ جَعَلْنَاكُمْ أُمَّةً وَسَطًا لِّتَكُونُوا شُهَدَاءَ عَلَى النَّاسِ وَيَكُونَ الرَّسُولُ عَلَيْكُمْ شَهِيدًا ۗ وَمَا جَعَلْنَا الْقِبْلَةَ الَّتِي كُنتَ عَلَيْهَا إِلَّا لِنَعْلَمَ مَن يَتَّبِعُ الرَّسُولَ مِمَّن يَنقَلِبُ عَلَىٰ عَقِبَيْهِ ۚ وَإِن كَانَتْ لَكَبِيرَةً إِلَّا عَلَى الَّذِينَ هَدَى اللَّهُ ۗ وَمَا كَانَ اللَّهُ لِيُضِيعَ إِيمَانَكُمْ ۚ إِنَّ اللَّهَ بِالنَّاسِ لَرَءُوفٌ رَّحِيمٌ ﴿١٤٣﴾ قَدْ نَرَىٰ تَقَلُّبَ وَجْهِكَ فِي السَّمَاءِ ۖ فَلَنُوَلِّيَنَّكَ قِبْلَةً تَرْضَاهَا ۚ فَوَلِّ وَجْهَكَ شَطْرَ الْمَسْجِدِ الْحَرَامِ ۚ وَحَيْثُ مَا كُنتُمْ فَوَلُّوا وُجُوهَكُمْ شَطْرَهُ ۗ وَإِنَّ الَّذِينَ أُوتُوا الْكِتَابَ لَيَعْلَمُونَ أَنَّهُ الْحَقُّ مِن رَّبِّهِمْ ۗ وَمَا اللَّهُ بِغَافِلٍ عَمَّا يَعْمَلُونَ ﴿١٤٤﴾

The foolish among the people will ask, "Why did they turn away from the direction of prayer they used to face?" Say, [O Prophet,] "The east and west belong [only] to Allah. He guides whoever He wills to the Straight Path." And so We have made you [believers] an upright community so that you may be witnesses over humanity and that the Messenger may be a witness over you. **We assigned your for-**

20 Al-Sijistānī, *Sunan Abī Dāwūd,* p. 337.

mer direction of prayer only to distinguish those who would remain faithful to the Messenger from those who would lose faith. It was certainly a difficult test except for those [rightly] guided by Allah. And Allah would never discount your [previous acts of] faith. Surely Allah is Ever Gracious and Most Merciful to humanity. **Indeed, We see you [O Prophet] turning your face towards heaven. Now We will make you turn towards a direction [of prayer] that will please you. So turn your face towards the Sacred Mosque [in Mecca]**—wherever you are, turn your faces towards it. Those who were given the Scripture certainly know this to be the truth from their Lord. And Allah is never unaware of what they do. (Q. 2:142-144)

Al-Barāʾ reports: "I prayed with the Prophet ﷺ towards Bayt al-Maqdis (in Jerusalem) for sixteen months till this verse of al-Baqarah was revealed:

وَحَيْثُ مَا كُنتُمْ فَوَلُّوا وُجُوهَكُمْ شَطْرَهُ ﴿١٤٤﴾

Wherever you are, turn your faces towards it. (Q. 2:144)

This verse was revealed after the Prophet ﷺ had prayed, so a man from among them passed by a group of the Anṣār, who were engaged in prayer, narrated to them this *ḥadīth*, and they turned their faces towards the House (in Makkah)."[21]

Like the previous verse, this one indicates the existence of non-Qurʾānic revelations, since the verse alludes to an earlier direction of prayer that isn't mentioned in the Qurʾān.

21 Al-Nīsāpūrī, *Ṣaḥīḥ Muslim*, p. 258.

In addition to these two verses, the sheer number of reports indicates that orders and prohibitions were narrated by the Companions. The third generation scholar Ibn al-Mubārak (d. 181 AH) estimated that the number of authentic *fiqh* narrations from the Prophet ﷺ were around nine hundred,[22] affirming a basis for much of what has been attributed to the Companions. After all, it would be unreasonable to assume that the second generation of Muslims colluded to falsely attribute reports on such a massive scale from their predecessors, especially when many of these reports are corroborated by multiple narrators from the Companion narrating it, as shown in *ḥadīths* earlier in the chapter.

Qur'ānism as a Sect

A verse often brought up by Qur'ānists is the following:

قُلْ هُوَ الْقَادِرُ عَلَىٰٓ أَن يَبْعَثَ عَلَيْكُمْ عَذَابًا مِّن فَوْقِكُمْ أَوْ مِن تَحْتِ
أَرْجُلِكُمْ أَوْ يَلْبِسَكُمْ شِيَعًا وَيُذِيقَ بَعْضَكُم بَأْسَ بَعْضٍ ۗ انظُرْ كَيْفَ
نُصَرِّفُ الْآيَاتِ لَعَلَّهُمْ يَفْقَهُونَ ﴿٦٥﴾

> Say, "He is the [one] Able to send upon you affliction from above you or from beneath your feet **or to confuse you [so you become] sects** and make you taste the violence of one another." Look how We diversify the signs that they might understand. (Q 6:65)

Qur'ānists often point to Sunnīs and Shī'as, claiming that these sects have emerged as a form of affliction from Allah the Almighty, and

---

22 Al-Sijistānī, *Risālat Abī Dāwūd ilā Ahl Makkah*, p. 27.

it is our duty to return to the Qur'ān alone, in order to not fall into sects. Ironically, both sects predate Qur'ānism. Ibn Sīrīn (d. 110 AH), a second generation scholar, references "*Ahlul Sunnah*" in a report,[23] while the earliest in which the Qur'ānists were alluded to as a group was by al-Shāfiʿī (d. 204 AH) a century later.[24] The early existence of *Ahlul Sunnah* should not come as a surprise after it has been established that the Companions of the Prophet ﷺ adhered to *ḥadīths* and narrated them. Furthermore, there were no Qur'ānists among them.

Classical works that list out the names of Islamic sects like al-Shahrastānī's *al-Milal wa al-Niḥal* and al-Baġdādī's *al-Farq bayn al-Firaq* don't make any mention of a Qur'ānist sect. Sh. Ṣalāḥ al-Dīn Maqbūl states that "the sects that emerged after the tribulations that occurred in the *ummah*, despite their number and diversity, didn't reject the *ḥadīths* in totality, but only partially. For example, the Khawārij rejected the *ḥadīths* of the merits of *Ahlul Bayt*, the Mu'tazilah rejected the *ḥadīths* of the attributes of Allah the Almighty, and the Shīʿah rejected the *ḥadīths* of the merits of the Companions ﷺ."[25] Despite the differences among all the early Muslim sects, they all recognized the necessity of *ḥadīth*.

Conclusion

While this may be hard to digest for the staunch Qur'ānist, there is no escaping the above arguments about the first generation of Muslims. Unfortunately, some may dismiss these matters as irrelevant,

23 Al-Nīsāpūrī, *Ṣaḥīḥ Muslim*, p. 51.
24 Al-Shāfiʿī, *al-Umm*, 2/2905.
25 Ahmad, *Zawābiʿ fī Wajh al-Sunnah*, p. 63.

claiming that historical accounts are irrelevant to them. However, a serious introspection will lead them to the undeniable fact that the Companions taught the generation that followed the religious rulings that they inherited from the Prophet ﷺ. Not a single one of them was anti-*ḥadīth*. This can only lead to the conclusion that the Prophet ﷺ instructed them to spread his teachings. We do not find the Companions quoting verses of the Qur'ān to condemn *ḥadīths* in the same way Qur'ānists do either.

Qur'ānists need to dig deep down and ask themselves: Is it possible that all these reports by the Companions were fabrications by them? Why would the best generation of Muslims, that were praised explicitly in the Qur'ān (Q. 9:100, 48:18, 48:29), collude to fabricate so many reports in the first place? Can we truly say that we understand Islam better than they do?

The Details of Prayer

Qur'ānists seem to differ in regards to how to approach prayer. Some are of the opinion that they should follow the masses since their actions are passed down from generation to generation, without being aware that doing so is a form of approval of the *sunnah*. However, this section is directed to those of the opinion that the Qur'ān is the only source for the actions of prayer, as well as Qur'ānists that reject the existence of a ritualistic prayer in the first place. Both positions can be debunked by familiarizing the Qur'ānist with aspects of prayer as recognized by the scholars of the first century.

A major point to keep in mind is the lack of a motive to introduce these acts. For instance, reports that speak of the merits of lands or people may be motivated by political allegiances. Reports about the merits of certain foods or trades may be financially motivated. Narrations that elaborate on ideological aspects of the religion may have originated due to sectarian motives. None of the above can be compared to the ritual prayer, and it is due to this that the following section will focus on aspects of the prayer, evidence for their prophetic origins, and their widespread adoption by first century figures.

The following lists of scholars are presented not only to affirm that these acts were observed by the Prophet ﷺ, but also to substantiate the claim that first century scholars, by consensus, adhered to *ḥadīths*.

Raising the Hands in the Beginning of Prayer

The following scholars held the opinion that hands should be raised at the start of prayer. This action cannot be found in the Qur'ān. It can be found in prophetic narrations and is a part of the prayer as per the consensus of all Muslims.[26]

Makkans:

- Ibn ʿAbbās (d. 68 AH)[27]
- Ibn al-Zubayr (d. 73 AH)[28]
- Al-Ḥasan bin Muslim (died after 100 AH)[29]
- Mujāhid (d. 104 AH)[30]
- ʿAtā' bin Abī Rabāḥ (d. 115 AH)[31]

Madīnans:

- ʿUmar (d. 23 AH)[32]

---

26 Ibn al-Mundir, *al-Ijmāʿ*, 31.

27 Al-Ṣanʿānī, *al-Muṣannaf*, 2/33; Ibn Abī Shayba, *al-Muṣannaf*, 1/212; Ibn al-Mundir, *al-Awsaṭ*, 3/301.

28 Al-Ṣanʿānī, *al-Muṣannaf*, 2/33; Ibn Abī Shayba, *al-Muṣannaf*, 1/212; Ibn al-Mundir, *al-Awsaṭ*, 3/301; Ibn ʿAbd al-Barr, *al-Tamhīd*, 5/67.

29 al-Kirmānī, *Masā'il Ḥarb bin Ismāʿīl al-Kirmānī*, p. 96.

30 Ibn Abī Shayba, *al-Muṣannaf*, 1/264; al-Kirmānī, *Masā'il Ḥarb bin Ismāʿīl al-Kirmānī*, p. 96.

31 Al-Ṣanʿānī, *al-Muṣannaf*, 2/33; al-Kirmānī, *Masā'il Ḥarb bin Ismāʿīl al-Kirmānī*, p. 96; Ibn Ḥazm, *al-Muḥallā*, p. 363.

32 Al-Ṣanʿānī, *al-Muṣannaf*, 2/34; Ibn Abī Shayba, *al-Muṣannaf*, 1/211; Ibn ʿAbd al-Barr, *al-Tamhīd*, 5/67.

- ʿUthmān (d. 35 AH)[33]
- Abū Hurayra (d. 59 AH)[34]
- Ibn ʿUmar (d. 74 AH)[35]
- Abū Saʿīd al-Khudrī (d. 74 AH)[36]
- Jābir bin ʿAbdillāh al-Anṣārī (d. 78 AH)[37]
- Sālim bin ʿAbdillāh bin ʿUmar (d. 106 AH)[38]
- Al-Qāsim bin Muḥammad bin Abī Bakr (d. 106 AH)[39]
- Nāfiʿ (d. 117 AH)[40]

Kūfans:

- Ibn Masʿūd (d. 32 AH)[41]
- Alī bin Abī Ṭālib (d. 40 AH)[42]

---

33 Al-Ṣanʿānī, *al-Muṣannaf*, 2/33. Ibn Ḥazm, *al-Muḥallā*, p. 363.
34 Ibn Abī Shayba, *al-Muṣannaf*, 1/212; al-Kirmānī, *Masāʾil Ḥarb bin Ismāʿīl al-Kirmānī*, p. 88-89.
35 Al-Ṣanʿānī, *al-Muṣannaf*, 2/32; Ibn Abī Shayba, *al-Muṣannaf*, 1/211; Al-Aṣbaḥī, *al-Muwaṭṭá*, p.59; Ibn al-Mundir, *al-Awsaṭ*, 3/301.
36 Ibn Abī Shayba, *al-Muṣannaf*, 1/212; Ibn al-Mundir, *al-Awsaṭ*, 3/301.
37 Ibn ʿAbd al-Barr, *al-Tamhīd*, 5/59.
38 Ibn Abī Shayba, *al-Muṣannaf*, 1/212; Ibn ʿAbd al-Barr, *al-Tamhīd*, 5/67.
39 Ibn ʿAbd al-Barr, *al-Tamhīd*, 5/67.
40 Al-Kirmānī, *Masāʾil Ḥarb bin Ismāʿīl al-Kirmānī*, p. 96; Ibn ʿAbd al-Barr, *al-Tamhīd*, 5/67.
41 Al-Ṣanʿānī, *al-Muṣannaf*, 2/34; Ibn Abī Shayba, *al-Muṣannaf*, 1/213.
42 Ibn Abī Shayba, *al-Muṣannaf*, 1/213.

- ʿAlqamah bin Qays (d. 62 AH)[43]
- Al-Aswad bin Yazīd (d. 75 AH)[44]
- Khaythamah bin ʿAbd al-Raḥmān (died after 80 AH)[45]
- ʿAbd al-Raḥmān bin Abī Laylā (d. 82 AH)[46]
- Ibrāhīm al-Nakhaʿī (d. 96 AH)[47]
- Qays bin Abī Ḥāzim (d. 98 AH)[48]
- Al-Shaʿbī (d. 104 AH)[49]

Baṣrans:

- Anas bin Mālik (d. 92 AH)[50]
- Abū Qilābah (d. 104 AH)[51]
- Ḥafṣah bint Sīrīn (died after 100 AH)[52]
- Muḥammad bin Sīrīn (d. 110 AH)[53]

---

43 Ibn Abī Shayba, *al-Muṣannaf*, 1/214.
44 Ibid.
45 Ibid.
46 Ibid.
47 Al-Ṣanʿānī, *al-Muṣannaf*, 2/34; Ibn Abī Shayba, *al-Muṣannaf*, 1/211; al-Kirmānī, *Masāʾil Ḥarb bin Ismāʿīl al-Kirmānī*, p. 87.
48 Ibn Abī Shayba, *al-Muṣannaf*, 1/214.
49 Ibid., 1/213.
50 Ibn Abī Shayba, *al-Muṣannaf*, 1/213; Ibn al-Mundir, *al-Awsaṭ*, 3/301.
51 Ibn Abī Shayba, *al-Muṣannaf*, 1/213.
52 Ibid., 1/216.
53 Ibn Abī Shayba, *al-Muṣannaf*, 1/213; al-Kirmānī, *Masāʾil Ḥarb bin*

- Qatādah (d. 110 AH)[54]
- Al-Ḥasan al-Baṣrī (d. 110 AH)[55]

Shāmīs:

- Umm al-Dardā' (d. 30 AH)[56]
- Makḥūl (d. 112 AH)[57]

Yemenis:

- Wahb bin Munabbih (d. 114 AH)[58]
- Ṭāwūs (d. 106 AH)[59]

This long list of scholars, all of whom lived in the first century of Islam and were from different regions, all held the view that the prayer should start off in the same manner, with the raising of the hands. More importantly, there is no alternative opinion that conflicts with this, as opposed to some other details revolving around the prayer. For example, we find multiple practices in regards to the placement of the hands during prayer. There are also differences of opinion as to whether the hands should be raised before and after bowing

Ismā'īl al-Kirmānī, p. 96.

54 Al-Ṣan'ānī, *al-Muṣannaf*, 2/90; al-Kirmānī, *Masā'il Ḥarb bin Ismā'īl al-Kirmānī*, p. 96.

55 Ibn Abī Shayba, *al-Muṣannaf*, 1/213; al-Kirmānī, *Masā'il Ḥarb bin Ismā'īl al-Kirmānī*, p. 96.

56 Ibn Abī Shayba, *al-Muṣannaf*, 1/216.

57 Ibn 'Abd al-Barr, *al-Tamhīd*, 5/67.

58 Al-Ṣan'ānī, *al-Muṣannaf*, 2/33; Ibn 'Abd al-Barr, *al-Tamhīd*, 5/66.

59 Al-Ṣan'ānī, *al-Muṣannaf*, 2/33; al-Kirmānī, *Masā'il Ḥarb bin Ismā'īl al-Kirmānī*, p. 96; Ibn 'Abd al-Barr, *al-Tamhīd*, 5/67.

in prayer. However, there is an absolute consensus in this specific matter, despite it not being included in the Qur'ān. Due to this, we can only arrive at one reasonable conclusion, which is that all these scholars learned to do this from the *ḥadīths* of the Prophet ﷺ.

It is also not a surprise to find a large number of reports, from the Companions of the Prophet ﷺ, all attributing this act to him. Al-Suyūṭī includes these reports in his collection of *mutawātir* transmissions, a term used to refer to reports that are too numerous in sources and chains to be concocted. He lists the following Companions as narrators for the report: Ibn ʿUmar, Mālik bin Ḥuwayrith, Wā'il bin Ḥujr, Alī, Sahl bin Sa'd, Ibn al-Zubayr, Ibn ʿAbbās, Muḥammad bin Maslamah, Abū Usayd, Abū Ḥumayd, Abū Qatāda, Abū Hurayrah, Anas, Jābir, ʿUmayr al-Laythī, al-Ḥakam bin ʿUmayr, Abū Bakr, al-Barā', ʿUmar bin al-Khaṭṭāb, Abū Mūsā al-Ashʿarī, ʿUqba bin ʿAmer, and Muʿāḏ bin Jabal.[60]

The *Tashahhud*

The *tashahhud,* another aspect of the ritual prayer, consists of a greeting followed by the testimony of faith. There is no mention of it in the Qur'ān, but the following scholars did not hesitate in making it a part of their prayer:

Makkans:

- Ibn ʿAbbās (d. 68 AH)[61]

60 Al-Suyūṭī, *Qaṭf al-Azhār al-Mutanāthira fī al-Akhbār al-Mutawātira,* p. 95-96.

61 Al-Ṣanʿānī, *al-Muṣannaf*, 2/87; Ibn Abī Shayba, *al-Muṣannaf*, 1/261.

- Ibn al-Zubayr (d. 73 AH)[62]
- Mujāhid (d. 104 AH)[63]
- ʿAtā' bin Abī Rabāḥ (d. 115 AH)[64]

Madīnans:

- Abū Bakr (d. 13 AH)[65]
- ʿUmar (d. 23 AH)[66]
- ʿĀ'ishah (d. 58 AH)[67]
- Ibn ʿUmar (d. 74 AH)[68]
- Abū Saʿīd al-Khudrī (d. 74 AH)[69]
- Nāfiʿ (d. 117 AH)[70]

Kūfans:

- Ibn Masʿūd (d. 32 AH)[71]

62 Al-Ṣanʿānī, *al-Muṣannaf*, 2/89.
63 Ibn Abī Shayba, *al-Muṣannaf*, 1/264.
64 Al-Ṣanʿānī, *al-Muṣannaf*, 2/87; Al-Ṭabarī, *Tahḏīb al-Āthār*, p. 252.
65 Ibn Abī Shayba, *al-Muṣannaf*, 1/260.
66 Al-Ṣanʿānī, *al-Muṣannaf*, 2/89; Ibn Abī Shayba, *al-Muṣannaf*, 1/261.
67 Al-Aṣbaḥī, *al-Muwaṭṭá*, p.66; Ibn Abī Shayba, *al-Muṣannaf*, 1/261.
68 Al-Ṣanʿānī, *al-Muṣannaf*, 2/89; Ibn Abī Shayba, *al-Muṣannaf*, 1/260.
69 Ibn Abī Shayba, *al-Muṣannaf*, 1/261; Al-Baġdādī, *Taqyīd al-ʿIlm*, p. 94.
70 Al-Ṣanʿānī, *al-Muṣannaf*, 2/91.
71 Al-Ṣanʿānī, *al-Muṣannaf*, 2/90; Ibn Abī Shayba, *al-Muṣannaf*, 1/262.

- ʿAlī bin Abī Ṭālib (d. 40 AH)[72]
- ʿAlqamah bin Qays (d. 62 AH)[73]
- Al-Rabīʿ bin Khuthaym (d. 65 AH)[74]
- Abū ʿAbd al-Raḥmān al-Sulamī (d. 74 AH)[75]
- Saʿīd bin Jubayr (d. 94 AH)[76]
- Ibrāhīm al-Nakhaʿī (d. 96 AH)[77]
- Muṣʿab bin Saʿd (d. 103 AH)[78]
- Al-Shaʿbī (d. 104 AH)[79]

Baṣrans:

- Muḥammad bin Sīrīn (d. 110 AH)[80]
- Al-Ḥasan al-Baṣrī (d. 110 AH)[81]

---

72 Al-Ṣanʿānī, *al-Muṣannaf*, 2/91.
73 Al-Ṣanʿānī, *al-Muṣannaf*, 2/88; Ibn Abī Shayba, *al-Muṣannaf*, 1/262; Al-Ṭabarānī, *al-Muʿjam al-Kabīr*, 7/2497.
74 Al-Ṣanʿānī, *al-Muṣannaf*, 2/88; Al-Ṭabarānī, *al-Muʿjam al-Kabīr*, 7/2497.
75 Ibn Abī Shayba, *al-Muṣannaf*, 1/262.
76 Al-Ṣanʿānī, *al-Muṣannaf*, 2/89.
77 Al-Ṣanʿānī, *al-Muṣannaf*, 2/90-91; Ibn Abī Shayba, *al-Muṣannaf*, 1/261; Al-Ṭabarī, *Tahḏīb al-Āthār*, p. 252.
78 Ibn Abī Shayba, *al-Muṣannaf*, 1/263-264.
79 Ibid., 1/263.
80 Al-Ṣanʿānī, *al-Muṣannaf*, 2/91; Ibn Abī Shayba, *al-Muṣannaf*, 1/261.
81 Al-Ṣanʿānī, *al-Muṣannaf*, 2/88-89; Al-Ṭabarī, *Tahḏīb al-Āthār*, p. 251.

- Qatādah (d. 110 AH)[82]

Shamīs:

- Makḥūl (d. 112 AH)[83]
- Sulaymān bin Mūsā (d. 119 AH)[84]

Yemenis:

- Ṭāwūs (d. 106 AH)[85]

Similar to the matter of raising the hands at the beginning of prayer, the *tashahhud* originated from the teachings of the Prophet ﷺ. Al-Suyūṭī lists the following Companions as having narrated that he ﷺ taught the *tashahhud*: Ibn Masʿūd, Ibn ʿAbbās, Abū Mūsā al-Ashʿarī, ʿUmar, Jābir, Ibn ʿUmar, Samurah bin Jundub, ʿĀ'ishah, ʿAlī, Ibn al-Zubayr, Muʿāwiyah bin Abī Sufyān, Salmān, Abū Ḥumayd, Abū Bakr al-Ṣiddīq, Ṭalḥah bin ʿUbaydillāh, Anas, Ḥudayfah, al-Ḥusayn bin ʿAlī, Ibn Abī Awfā, al-Faḍl bin al-ʿAbbās, Abū Saʿīd, Abū Hurayrah, and Umm Salama.[86]

One notable detail about the *tashahhud* is that it has been reported in various, albeit similar, wordings. Ibn al-Mundir states that Imam Aḥmad and the scholars of *al-rải* would recite Ibn Masʿūd's wording, Imam Mālik and the people of Madinah recited ʿUmar's word-

82 Al-Ṣanʿānī, *al-Muṣannaf*, 2/90.
83 Al-Ṭabarī, *Tahḏīb al-Āthār*, p. 251.
84 Ibid.
85 Al-Ṣanʿānī, *al-Muṣannaf*, 2/87; Al-Ṭabarī, *Tahḏīb al-Āthār*, p. 252.
86 Al-Suyūṭī, *Qaṭf al-Azhār al-Mutanāthira fī al-Akhbār al-Mutawātira*, p. 98.

ing, and al-Shāfiʿī recited Ibn ʿAbbās' wording.[87] Imam Aḥmad further states that he prefers the *tashahhud* of Ibn Masʿūd even though he believes that all of them are permissible and that the different versions of the *tashahhud* were taught by the Prophet ﷺ himself.[88] The Qur'ānist is free to be skeptical about the variants in the *tashahhud*, perhaps even using it as evidence that it was not preserved verbatim. For the sake of the argument, even if that was the case, the Qur'ānist is still left unable to explain the origins of three established renditions of the *tashahhud* in the first place. Furthermore, the existence of variants will undermine any possible claims of them being late fabrications, for if they were fabrications, there would be more uniformity instead of diversity.

The *Taslīm*

The *taslīm* is the act at the end of the ritual prayer in which one turns their head and says: "*As-salāmu ʿalaykum wa raḥmatullāh.*" Classical scholars, from as early as the first century, affirmed that this act is a part of the prayer, but differed as to whether the Prophet ﷺ did it once to the right or with an additional turn to the left. Like the previous example of the *tashahhud*, the existence of varying opinions undermines theories about the *taslīm* being a late invention.

The following is a list of first century scholars that affirmed that the *taslīm* is a part of the prayer:

Makkans:

---

87 Ibn al-Mundir, *al-Awsaṭ min al-Sunan wal-Ijmāʿ wal-Ikhtilāf*, 3/376-377.
88 Al-Maqdisī, *al-Mugnī*, 1/220.

- Ibn ʿAbbās (d. 68 AH)[89]
- Nāfiʿ bin ʿAbd al-Ḥārith[90]
- ʿAtā' bin Abī Rabāḥ (d. 115 AH)[91]

Madīnans:

- Abū Bakr (d. 13 AH)[92]
- ʿUmar (d. 23 AH)[93]
- Abū Ḏar (d. 32 AH)[94]
- ʿUthmān (d. 35 AH)[95]
- ʿAmmār bin Yāsir (d. 37 AH)[96]
- Zayd bin Thābit (d. 45 AH)[97]
- ʿĀ'ishah (d. 58 AH)[98]

---

89 Al-Haythamī, *Buġyat al-Bāḥith ʿan Zawā'id Musnad al-Ḥārith*, 1/292.
90 Al-Ṣanʿānī, *al-Muṣannaf*, 2/96.
91 Ibid.
92 Al-Ṣanʿānī, *al-Muṣannaf*, 2/97; Ibn Abī Shayba, *al-Muṣannaf*, 1/267; Al-Jurjānī, *al-Kāmil*, 2/195.
93 Al-Ṣanʿānī, *al-Muṣannaf*, 2/95; Ibn Abī Shayba, *al-Muṣannaf*, 1/266; Al-Jurjānī, *al-Kāmil*, 2/195; Al-Haythamī, *Buġyat al-Bāḥith ʿan Zawā'id Musnad al-Ḥārith*, 1/292.
94 Al-Haythamī, *Buġyat al-Bāḥith ʿan Zawā'id Musnad al-Ḥārith*, 1/292.
95 Al-Ṣanʿānī, *al-Muṣannaf*, 2/97; Al-Jurjānī, *al-Kāmil*, 2/195.
96 Al-Ṣanʿānī, *al-Muṣannaf*, 2/96; Ibn Abī Shayba, *al-Muṣannaf*, 1/266.
97 Al-Haythamī, *Buġyat al-Bāḥith ʿan Zawā'id Musnad al-Ḥārith*, 1/292.
98 Ibn Abī Shayba, *al-Muṣannaf*, 1/268; Al-Nīsāpūrī, *Ṣaḥīḥ Muslim*, p. 282-283; Ibn Khuzayma, *Ṣaḥīḥ Ibn Khuzayma*, 1/382.

- Ibn ʿUmar (d. 74 AH)[99]
- ʿUrwah bin al-Zubayr (d. 93 AH)[100]
- Saʿīd bin al-Musayyib (d. 94 AH)[101]
- Khārijah bin Zayd (d. 96 AH)[102]
- ʿUmar bin ʿAbd al-ʿAzīz (d. 101 AH)[103]

Kūfans:

- Ibn Masʿūd (d. 32 AH)[104]
- ʿAlī bin Abī Ṭālib (d. 40 AH)[105]
- ʿAlqamah bin Qays (d. 62 AH)[106]
- Masrūq (d. 63 AH)[107]
- Abū ʿAbd al-Raḥmān al-Sulamī (d. 74 AH)[108]

---

99 Al-Ṣanʿānī, *al-Muṣannaf*, 2/97; Ibn Abī Shayba, *al-Muṣannaf*, 1/266.
100 Ibn Khuzayma, *Ṣaḥīḥ Ibn Khuzayma*, 1/382.
101 Al-Aṣbaḥī, *al-Mudawwana al-Kubrā*, 2/226; Ibn Abī Shayba, *al-Muṣannaf*, 1/273.
102 Al-Aṣbaḥī, *al-Mudawwana al-Kubrā*, 2/226.
103 Al-Ṣanʿānī, *al-Muṣannaf*, 2/97; Ibn ʿAsākir, *Tārīkh Dimashq*, 8/449.
104 Al-Ṣanʿānī, *al-Muṣannaf*, 2/96.
105 Al-Ṣanʿānī, *al-Muṣannaf*, 2/96; Ibn Abī Shayba, *al-Muṣannaf*, 1/266; Ibn Saʿd, *al-Ṭabaqāt al-Kabīr*, 8/296; Al-Haythamī, *Buġyat al-Bāḥith ʿan Zawāʾid Musnad al-Ḥārith*, 1/292.
106 Ibn Abī Shayba, *al-Muṣannaf*, 1/266.
107 Ibid., 1/267.
108 Ibid., 1/266.

- ʿAmr bin Maymūn (d. 75 AH)[109]
- Al-Aswad bin Yazīd (d. 75 AH)[110]
- Jābir bin Samurah (d. 76 AH)[111]
- Khaythamah bin ʿAbd al-Raḥmān (died after 80 AH)[112]
- Suwayd bin Ġafalah (d. 81 AH)[113]
- Abū Wāʾel (d. 82 AH)[114]
- ʿAbd al-Raḥmān bin Abī Laylā (d. 82 AH)[115]
- ʿAbdullāh bin Abī Awfā (d. 86 AH)[116]
- Saʿīd bin Jubayr (d. 94 AH)[117]
- Ibrāhīm al-Nakhaʿī (d. 96 AH)[118]
- Qays bin Abī Ḥāzim (d. 98 AH)[119]
- Yaḥyā bin Waththāb (d. 103 AH)[120]

---

109 Ibid., 1/267.
110 Ibid., 1/266.
111 Al-Ṣanʿānī, *al-Muṣannaf*, 2/96; al-Ṭabarānī, *al-Muʿjam al-Kabīr*, 2/486.
112 Ibn Abī Shayba, *al-Muṣannaf*, 1/266.
113 Ibid., 1/268.
114 Ibid., 1/267.
115 Ibid., 1/266.
116 Ibid., 1/268.
117 Ibid.
118 Ibid., 1/266.
119 Ibid., 1/268.
120 Ibid., 1/267.

Baṣrans:

- Anas bin Mālik (d. 92 AH)[121]
- Abū al-ʿĀliyah (d. 93 AH)[122]
- Abū Qilābah (d. 104 AH)[123]
- Abū Rajāʾ (d. 105 AH)[124]
- Muḥammad bin Sīrīn (d. 110 AH)[125]
- Al-Ḥasan al-Baṣrī (d. 110 AH)[126]
- Qatādah (d. 110 AH)[127]

Shāmī:

- Qabīṣah bin Ḏuʾayb (d. 82 AH)[128]

As for the narrations of the Prophet ﷺ, we find al-Suyūṭī listing out the following Companions as narrators of *ḥadīths* on this topic: Saʿd bin Abī Waqqās, Jābir bin Samura, Wāel bin Ḥujr, Ibn Masʿūd, ʿAmmar bin Yāsir, Ḥuḏayfah, ʿAdī bin ʿAmīrah, Sahl bin Saʿd, Ṭalq bin ʿAlī, al-Muġīrah bin Shuʿbah, Abū Rimtha, Wāthila bin al-Asqaʿ,

---

121 Ibid.
122 Ibid., 1/268.
123 Al-Ṣanʿānī, *al-Muṣannaf*, 2/96-97.
124 Ibn Abī Shayba, *al-Muṣannaf*, 1/268.
125 Al-Ṣanʿānī, *al-Muṣannaf*, 2/96-97; Ibn Abī Shayba, *al-Muṣannaf*, 1/267.
126 Al-Ṣanʿānī, *al-Muṣannaf*, 2/97; Ibn Abī Shayba, *al-Muṣannaf*, 1/267.
127 Al-Ṣanʿānī, *al-Muṣannaf*, 2/97.
128 Al-Haythamī, *Buġyat al-Bāḥith ʿan Zawāʾid Musnad al-Ḥārith*, 1/293.

al-Barāʾ bin ʿĀzib, and Yaʿqūb bin al-Ḥuṣayn.[129] In light of the abundance of these narrations, it is only natural to assume that they led to the adoption of the *taslīm* by the first century scholars above.

Conclusion

We need to keep in mind that there is no objective reason for the rejection of these attributions to classical scholars, for their opinions are not binding upon us. However, it naturally leads down a line of questioning: Why did they hold these opinions in the first place if they cannot be found in the Qurʾān? The raising of the hands at the start of prayer, the *tashahhud*, and the *taslīm*, are a part of the ritual prayer that do not have any political, sectarian, ideological, or financial motivations tied to them. Since so many first century scholars observed these acts, it is only natural to conclude that they only did so because they followed the *ḥadīths* of the Prophet ﷺ. Had a Qurʾān-only movement existed in the early generations of Islam, one would expect to find proponents of that ideology dismissing these acts as innovations.

129 Al-Suyūṭī, *Qaṭf al-Azhār al-Mutanāthira fī al-Akhbār al-Mutawātira*, p. 104.

Verses Used by Qur'ānists

While the Qur'ānist's qualms with *ḥadīth* have to do with the *ḥadīths* themselves, this did not stop them from developing arguments from the Qur'ān in order to support their position. Most of the verses used to argue for a Qur'ān-only Islam are entirely irrelevant to the claims of Qur'ānists, so only the most relevant verses for their case will be dealt with in this section.

Verses that Condemn *Ḥadīth*

أَوَلَمْ يَنظُرُوا فِي مَلَكُوتِ السَّمَاوَاتِ وَالْأَرْضِ وَمَا خَلَقَ اللَّهُ مِن شَيْءٍ وَأَنْ
عَسَىٰ أَن يَكُونَ قَدِ اقْتَرَبَ أَجَلُهُمْ ۖ فَبِأَيِّ حَدِيثٍ بَعْدَهُ يُؤْمِنُونَ ﴿١٨٥﴾

> Do they not look into the realm of the heavens and the earth and everything that Allah has created and [think] that perhaps their appointed time has come near? **So in what *ḥadīth* hereafter will they believe**? (Q. 7:185)

This verse and others like it (Q. 45:6, 77:50) indicate a condemnation of "*ḥadīth*," and thus, Qur'ānists make the claim that the verse denounces prophetic narrations. These verses are the bread and butter of most Qur'ān-only arguments, mainly due to the shock factor that comes with finding the term "*ḥadīth*" within a verse.

Qur'ānists conflate the word "*ḥadīth*" meaning "statement" in the verse, with the "prophetic *ḥadīths*" that we are all used to today.

This is not the intention of the verse at all. Plus, if taken literally, it would mean that all "*ḥadīths*/statements" are false. Are we to assume that every statement made by the creation is false? Naturally, the verse isn't condemning all non-Qurānic statements, but rather, it is rebuking disbelievers for their rejection of the statements and declarations of their Lord.

Al-Ṭabarī (d. 310 AH) explains:

> The Almighty says: Didn't those that disbelieve in the signs of their Lord look upon His kingdom and dominion in the heavens and the earth, and His creation within them, to contemplate and consider that there is no equal or anything like Him? Those who have done this should not worship anyone but Him. So they need to believe in Him, accept His messenger, and move towards obeying him, detach themselves from the deities and idols. They should be careful for their time is near. They may die upon their disbelief and end up in the punishment of Allah.
>
> As for His statement: "So in what *ḥadīth* hereafter will they believe?" He is saying: Then what sort of warning and admonition after the warning of Muḥammad ﷺ that he has brought to you from Allah through the verses of His book will you believe in if you did not believe in this book that Muḥammad ﷺ brought to you from Allah the Almighty?[130]

Everything is in the Qur'ān

Perhaps the second most common type of verses mentioned by

130 Al-Ṭabarī, *Tafsīr al-Ṭabarī*, 6/135.

Qur'ānists are those that speak of the Qur'ān being detailed, implying that the *sunnah* is not needed for details.

Verse 1

وَمَا مِن دَابَّةٍ فِي الْأَرْضِ وَلَا طَائِرٍ يَطِيرُ بِجَنَاحَيْهِ إِلَّا أُمَمٌ أَمْثَالُكُم ۚ مَّا فَرَّطْنَا فِي الْكِتَابِ مِن شَيْءٍ ۚ ثُمَّ إِلَىٰ رَبِّهِمْ يُحْشَرُونَ ﴿٣٨﴾

> There is not a moving creature on earth, nor a bird that flies with its two wings, but are communities like you. **We have neglected nothing in the Book**, then unto their Lord they shall be gathered. (Q. 6:38)

The bolded section of the verse is taken out of context by Qur'ānists. Their understanding wouldn't make much sense, if the context was taken into consideration. Why would a verse refer to beasts and birds as communities, then suggest that the Qur'ān contains all things, then state that the beasts and birds will be gathered on the Day of Judgment? This disconnect in meaning is due to the misinterpretation of the "book" mentioned in the verse. It is not referring to the Qur'ān. Qatādah (d. 110 AH) explains: "**We have neglected nothing in the Book**," is referring to the Book that is with Him.[131] In other words, the verse speaks of the communities of animals and states that their actions are recorded, and just like mankind, they will be gathered in the hereafter.

131 Al-Ṣanʿānī, *Tafsīr Abd al-Razzāq*, 2/47.

Verse 2

> Most surely, in their narrative there has been a lesson for people of understanding. This was not a fabricated ***ḥadīth***, but a confirmation of what came before it and a **detailed explanation of everything** and guidance and mercy for people who believe. (Q. 12:111)

The argument is straightforward in this verse. The Qur'ān is a "detailed explanation of everything" and therefore nothing more is needed. However, the Qur'ān is not even mentioned in the verse. This understanding is only possible if the word "this," underlined above, is referring to the Qur'ān. However, it seems that "this" is referring to the story of Yusuf since it is the most detailed narrative that we find in the Qur'ān. Also, refer to verse 4 below.

Verse 3

أَفَغَيْرَ اللَّهِ أَبْتَغِي حَكَمًا وَهُوَ الَّذِي أَنزَلَ إِلَيْكُمُ الْكِتَابَ مُفَصَّلًا ۚ وَالَّذِينَ آتَيْنَاهُمُ الْكِتَابَ يَعْلَمُونَ أَنَّهُ مُنَزَّلٌ مِّن رَّبِّكَ بِالْحَقِّ ۖ فَلَا تَكُونَنَّ مِنَ الْمُمْتَرِينَ ﴿١١٤﴾

> "Shall I seek a judge other than Allah and He is One who sent down the Book *mufaṣṣalan*?" And those that were given the Scripture know that it is revealed from your Lord with truth. So do not be one of those who doubt. (Q. 6:114)

The argument is similar to the previous verse, with the exception that this verse is clearly referring to the Qur'ān. It is also based on the understanding of the term "*mufaṣṣalan.*" Qatādah explains that the term "*mufaṣṣalan*" means "that which is made clear."

Qatādah explains: "The book *mufaṣṣalan*, (Q. 6:114)" means that it was made clear. When He said, "*Yufaṣṣilu* His *āyāt*, (Q. 10:5)" He means that He makes His *āyāt* clear. When He says, "*Faṣṣala* what is prohibited onto you, (Q. 6:119)" He means that He made what is prohibited onto you clear.[132] The understanding of Qatāda is echoed in classical dictionaries like *Tahḏīb al-Luġa* and *al-Qāmūs al-Muḥīt*.[133] There is no doubt that much of the Qur'ān is clear, however, that doesn't mean that revelation is restricted to the Qur'ān. Anyone that makes such claims would need to provide explicit evidence.

Verse 4

وَيَوْمَ نَبْعَثُ فِي كُلِّ أُمَّةٍ شَهِيدًا عَلَيْهِم مِّنْ أَنفُسِهِمْ ۖ وَجِئْنَا بِكَ شَهِيدًا عَلَىٰ هَٰؤُلَاءِ ۚ وَنَزَّلْنَا عَلَيْكَ الْكِتَابَ تِبْيَانًا لِّكُلِّ شَيْءٍ وَهُدًى وَرَحْمَةً وَبُشْرَىٰ لِلْمُسْلِمِينَ ﴿٨٩﴾

> And on the Day when We will resurrect among every nation a witness over them from themselves. And We will bring you, as a witness over these. **And We have sent down to you the Book as clarification for all things** and as guidance and mercy and good tidings for the Muslims. (Q. 16:89)

The verse is used to imply that every ruling in Islam is explicitly men-

132 Al-Ṣan'ānī, *Tafsīr Abd al-Razzāq*, 2/47.
133 Al-Azharī, *Mu'jam Tahḏīb al-Luġa*, 3/2795; al-Fayrūzābādī, al-Qāmūs al-Muḥīt, p. 1043.

tioned in the Qur'ān due to the clarification being "for all things." However, the usage of "*kul shay'* (all things)" is often used as a hyperbole in Arabic and even in the Qur'ān.

إِنِّي وَجَدتُّ امْرَأَةً تَمْلِكُهُمْ وَأُوتِيَتْ مِن كُلِّ شَيْءٍ وَلَهَا عَرْشٌ عَظِيمٌ ﴿٢٣﴾

Indeed, I found a woman ruling them, and she has been given of **all things**, and she has a great throne. (Q. 27:23)

تُدَمِّرُ كُلَّ شَيْءٍ بِأَمْرِ رَبِّهَا فَأَصْبَحُوا لَا يُرَىٰ إِلَّا مَسَاكِنُهُمْ ۚ كَذَٰلِكَ نَجْزِي الْقَوْمَ الْمُجْرِمِينَ ﴿٢٥﴾

Destroying **everything** by command of its Lord. And they became so that nothing was seen except their dwellings. Thus, do We recompense the criminal people. (Q. 46:25)

وَقَالُوا إِن نَّتَّبِعِ الْهُدَىٰ مَعَكَ نُتَخَطَّفْ مِنْ أَرْضِنَا ۚ أَوَلَمْ نُمَكِّن لَّهُمْ حَرَمًا آمِنًا يُجْبَىٰ إِلَيْهِ ثَمَرَاتُ كُلِّ شَيْءٍ رِّزْقًا مِّن لَّدُنَّا وَلَٰكِنَّ أَكْثَرَهُمْ لَا يَعْلَمُونَ ﴿٥٧﴾

And they say, "If we were to follow the guidance with you, we would be swept from our land." Have We not established for them a safe sanctuary to which are brought the fruits of **all things** as provision from Us? But most of them do not know. (Q. 28:57)

It goes without saying that the Queen of Sheba didn't literally possess everything, the wind didn't literally destroy the Earth in its totality, nor was every single type of fruit brought to Makkah.

Furthermore, we find the same hyperbole elsewhere in a verse about the tablets of Mūsā:

وَكَتَبْنَا لَهُ فِي الْأَلْوَاحِ مِن كُلِّ شَيْءٍ مَّوْعِظَةً وَتَفْصِيلًا لِّكُلِّ شَيْءٍ فَخُذْهَا بِقُوَّةٍ
وَأْمُرْ قَوْمَكَ يَأْخُذُوا بِأَحْسَنِهَا ۚ سَأُرِيكُمْ دَارَ الْفَاسِقِينَ ﴿١٤٥﴾

> And We wrote for him on the tablets of **all things** - instruction and explanation for all things, "Take them with determination and order your people to take the best of it. I will show you the home of the defiantly disobedient." (Q. 7:145)

Of course, we find several verses in the Qur'ān in which Mūsā is providing orders to the Jews that were not found in the tablet (Q. 2:67-71). Those revelations are like the *sunnah* in the sense that they are revealed outside of the written text even though the text says that it clarifies or explains "all things." Hence, this phrase should not be taken literally.[134]

When was the Qur'ān Fully Detailed?

If we accepted the claim, for the sake of the argument, that the Qur'ān was literally fully detailed, a question that needs to be posed is: When did it become fully detailed? The answer to the question itself will dispel the argument.

Two possible answers come to mind: 1) Upon the completion of the revelation of the Qur'ān as a whole, or 2) upon the revelation of the verses that state that the Qur'ān is fully detailed.

The problem with both theories is that they conflict with the reality

---

134 Credit goes to Jake Brancatella for this solid response.

of the Qur'ān. The four verses used in the section above are all from Makkan chapters of the Qur'ān, meaning that much of the Qur'ān was yet to be revealed. In other words, the Qur'ān was referred to as "fully detailed" before the completion of the full revelation.

If someone argued for the second theory, at most it would mean that the Qur'ān was "fully detailed" for that specific period. In other words, a few years later, the Qur'ān couldn't be considered literally "fully detailed" at the period of revelation, since more was added to it. Take for example, the verse of ablution in Sūrat al-Mā'ida, which was the last chapter revealed. If the Qur'ān was "fully detailed" before the revelation of the chapter, why didn't it include the method of ablution? Therefore, we need to accept that "fully detailed" here is only hyperbole since more religious rulings were added after these verses. However, since this is the case, there should be no contentions to additional revelation after the above verses were revealed, even if they come in the form of *ḥadīths*.

The only argument that a Qur'ānist may present is that we don't know if these three chapters (Q. 6, 12, 16) were Makkan, and that it is possible that these were all revealed very late in the time of the Prophet ﷺ. The response to this would simply be that there is a consensus among all scholars regarding these chapters being Makkan. Ibn 'Abbās, Jābir bin Zayd, 'Alī bin Abī Ṭalḥah, al-Zuhrī, the teachers of Yaḥyā bin Sallām al-Baṣrī, Abū al-Qāsim al-Nīṣāpūrī, and Ibn Shayṭā, agree that Sūrat al-An'ām (Q. 6) was revealed in Makkah.[135] In addition to the previous scholars, Ibn al-Zubayr, 'Ikrimah, al-Ḥasan, and Qatādah, all agree that Sūrat Yūsuf (Q. 12) was revealed

135 Aḥmad, *al-Makkī wal-Madanī fī al-Qur'ān al-Karīm*, 1/304-305.

in Makkah.[136] As for Sūrat al-Naḥl (Q. 16), all of the previous scholars also agreed that it was revealed in Makkah,[137] with the exception of Qatādah and Jābir bin Zayd, who said that the last forty verses in the chapter were revealed in Madīnah. While this is a matter of dispute among scholars of the Qur'ān, it doesn't matter much since two of these chapters were definitely revealed in Makkah, which solidifies the argument.

I would like to emphasize that the positions held by these scholars are not based upon any agenda, for they surely did not foresee my usage of their statements as evidence for the necessity of *ḥadīth*.

Also, these positions cannot be dismissed as baseless conjecture. These are the experts in the field, some of whom are from the first century. Furthermore, their collective testimony surely outweighs the biases of a Qur'ānist, whose opinion is based on a reaction; one that didn't even exist prior to reading this chapter.

Conclusion

The verses used by Qur'ānist to push for their position are irrelevant to the historical context of revelation. When the Qur'ān was directing a stern warning against unbelievers for their rejection of monotheism and the Day of Judgment, the last thing that would come to mind would be an order, to polytheists, towards rejection of the *ḥadīths*. Why provide them such an instruction in the first place when they don't even believe in the Qur'ān? When Qur'ānists make such argument, it not only displays how disconnected they

136 Ibid., 1/337-338.
137 Ibid., 1/355-357.

are from the context of the Qur'ān, but also how they are pushing, intentionally or not, their biases onto the verses.

The Qur'ānist's Objections to the System

While Qur'ānist mainly use verses in order to argue for their position, objections towards the *ḥadīth* system are a common tactic that they employ. After all, if the *ḥadīths* are all unreliable, then it wouldn't make much sense to adhere to them, regardless of whether the Qur'ān endorses them or not.

Objection 1: Documentation Was Two-Hundred Years Too Late

The argument about late documentation is perhaps the most oft-repeated one. The assumption by both soft and staunch Qur'ānists is that *ḥadīths* were first documented by al-Bukhārī and Muslim after year two hundred, and therefore, cannot be relied upon.

The claim demonstrates the ignorance of the Qur'ānist since documentation existed very early on in Islam, even since the time of Muḥammad ﷺ. In a narration, he allows ʿAbdullāh bin ʿAmr bin al-ʿĀṣ to document everything he says.[138] In another, he orders the Companions to document his sermon to Abū Shāh.[139] We also have

---

138 Al-Sijistānī, *Sunan Abī Dāwūd*, pp. 523-524.

139 Al-Nīsāpūrī, *Ṣaḥīḥ Muslim*, pp. 613-614. Qur'ānists sometimes make the ironic claim that Abū Saʿīd al-Khudrī narrated a prohibition to document *ḥadīths*. While this seems to be the case, traditional scholars have reconciled these reports by saying that this was because only the Qur'ān should be written, but this ruling was abrogated by the hadith of ʿAbdullāh bin ʿAmr bin

many examples of the first generation of Muslims documenting *ḥadīths*, including the caliphs, Abū Bakr[140] and ʿUmar.[141] Dr. Azami collects a list of over fifty companions that documented *ḥadīths* while providing references from classical sources.[142] Even though most of these works are no longer extant, we do have the *ṣaḥīfah* of Hammām, the student of Abū Hurayrah (d. 59 AH), containing 139 narrations, which was published by Dār al-Khānjī in Cairo in 1985.

Also, as established previously, second century works like Mālik's *Muwaṭṭá* preserve many traditions through only two narrators. So, even though Mālik's temporal distance from the Prophet ﷺ is quite long, his situation is not different from many contemporaries of the Prophet ﷺ that were separated by a physical distance, like first generation Muslims from Yemen or Bahrain. After all, the Prophet ﷺ did not make it obligatory for Yemenis to learn the Qur'ān and *sunnah* from him directly. Instead, he sent Muʿāḏ to Yemen to teach them Islam.[143] Obviously, a single man wasn't enough to teach the entire population of Yemen, which would have been over a hundred thousand at the time. This would mean that an educated tribesman that learned from Muʿāḏ would return home to teach his own people.

---

al-ʿĀṣ and Abū Shāh. This is overwhelmingly supported by the fact that the Companions documented hadiths. If a prohibition was always implemented, then none of them would be documenting hadiths in the first place. Moreover, the *ḥadīth* of Abū Saʿīd shouldn't be utilized by Qur'ānists since 1) it is a *ḥadīth* and 2) it actually instructs the Companions to narrate *ḥadīths* without documenting them.

140 Ibn Ḥanbal, *Musnad Aḥmad*, pp. 16-17.

141 Ibid., p. 33.

142 Azami, *Dirāsāt fī al-Ḥadīth al-Nabawī*, pp. 92-142.

143 Al-Nīsāpūrī, *Ṣaḥīḥ Muslim*, p. 72.

Hence, in many cases, there were two degrees of separation between many Yemenis and the Prophet ﷺ. That separation was caused by distance, while Mālik's separation was through time.

For the sake of the argument, even if we assumed that oral transmission was the only mode of transmission for two hundred years, it still wouldn't mean that it was unreliable. In fact, at times, oral transmission would be preferred over documented reports. For example, *ḥadīth* critic Ibn Maʿīn preferred the reports that Suwayd bin Saʿīd memorized over what he documented.[144] This is because when Suwayd lost his sight, people narrated his reports to him from his book, which he would confirm even though the information wasn't his own. However, he wouldn't make that mistake when narrating from memory. In this specific scenario, oral transmission was preferred over documentation, and the modern Qur'ānist would have relied upon unreliable reports due to the assumption that documentation necessitates accuracy.

Objection 2: al-Bukhārī is Unreliable

The arguments made against al-Bukhārī specifically are diverse. Some Qur'ānists suggest that he fabricated *ḥadīths* himself. Others argue that he didn't know Arabic. Some suggested that he organized a Persian conspiracy to destroy Islam from within.

Of course, these are nothing more than baseless claims that don't affect the veracity of his work and his reliability as a compiler of *ḥadīths*. The burden of proof is upon those that make these allegations. Moreover, all the reports of al-Bukhārī can be found in

144 Al-Baġdādī, *Tārīkh Baġdād*, 9/229.

other works. By comparing al-Bukhārī's book to Muslim's alone, we find that al-Bukhārī only relates 813 reports that aren't available in Muslim's compilation,[145] let alone all the other books of *ḥadīth*. Furthermore, there are supplementary works that corroborate the narrations of al-Bukhārī from cover to cover, which are referred to as *mustakhrajāt*. A few of them are available in printed form, like the *Mustakhraj* of Abū Nuʿaym al-Aṣbahānī, *Jāmiʿ al-Ṣaḥīḥayn* by al-Ḥaddād, and *Mustakhraj* al-Bujayrī. The *Mustakhraj* of al-Milanjī is available too, but only in manuscript form in the Ẓāhirīyyah Library in Damascus. In other words, even if everyone decided to denounce al-Bukhārī as unreliable, it would have no effect on his *ḥadīths* since they are all reported by others.

Take for example the *ḥadīth* in which al-Bukhārī narrated from Sahl bin Saʿd that "a drink was brought to the Messenger ﷺ when on his right was a boy and on his left were some old men. So he said to the boy: 'Would you permit me to give it to them?' The boy said, 'No, by Allah, I prefer that none get my portion from you.' So he placed it in the boy's hand."[146]

The same exact report is narrated by Abū Nuʿaym in his *Mustakhraj*, through his path, to the teacher of al-Bukhārī.[147]

145 Al-Ḥajūrī, *Talbiyat al-Amānī bi-Afrād al-Imām al-Bukhārī*, p. 489.
146 Al-Bukhārī, *Ṣaḥīḥ al-Bukhārī*, p. 421.
147 Al-Aṣbahānī, *al-Mustakhraj ʿalā Ṣaḥīḥ al-Bukhārī*, p. 308.

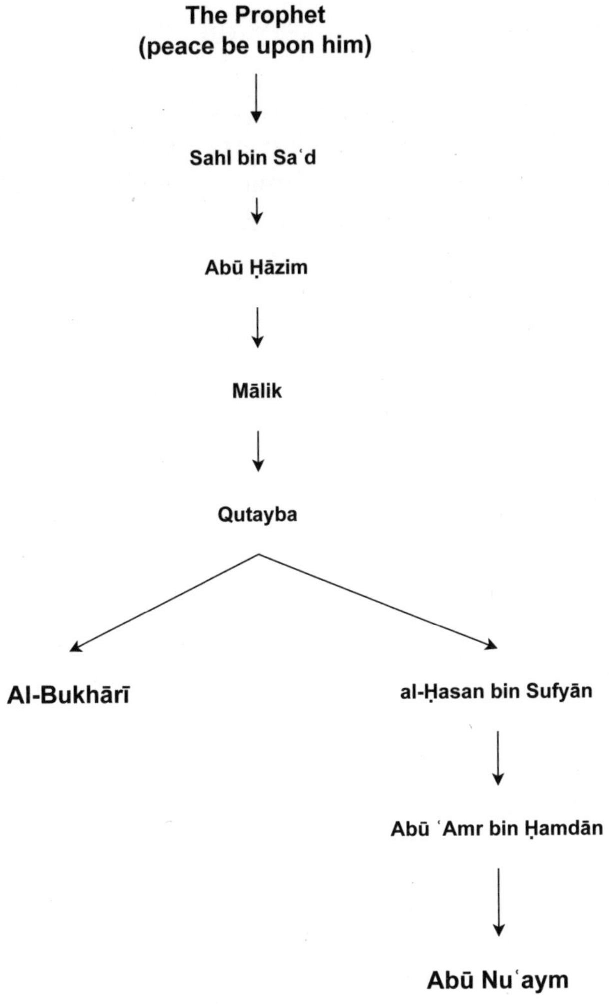

Objection 3: Manuscripts aren't Originals

A strange demand that may be made by the desperate Qur'ānist is that none of the books of *ḥadīth* are authoritative since much of the classical texts are based on copies and not the originals. The argument isn't well-thought out and is quickly rebutted by the fact that we don't have the original copy of the Qur'ān either. Instead, we only have access to copies of ʿUthmān's *maṣāḥif* that were sent to the regions. If Qur'ānists were consistent, they would need to reject the Qur'ān as well. However, the Qur'ān is preserved through multiple manuscripts that attest to one another, the *rasm* literature, and the *qirā'āt,* which will be covered in the next chapter.

Moreover, no serious student of history, Muslim or not, ever demanded the original manuscript to consider a work authentic. Demanding as much is merely an excuse to reject the authority of these works. It wouldn't be a surprise if a Qur'ānist denied the authority of these works even if they existed, perhaps claiming that we can't be sure if these texts were indeed written by their authors.

Ḥadīth works, like the Qur'ān, are published while relying on multiple manuscripts which attest to each other, and are supported by secondary sources that quote them. The reports that they contain are corroborated by other *ḥadīth* works as well. Hence, the need to discard *ḥadīths* due to this objection is a baseless and overblown reaction that is driven by the desire to reject *ḥadīths*.

Objection 4: Chinese Whispers

The Chinese Whispers argument is not the brightest argument by *ḥadīth* rejecters, but a common one nonetheless. Basically, the argument is that the narrators in the chain are similar to participants in a game of Chinese Whispers in which a group of people stand in a line with each of them whispering a message into the ear of the person beside them. At the end, the message often turns out to be distorted from the original.

The analogy is a horrible one and can easily be countered with the following question: What if the game was played with two lines of people, independent from one another, and both produced the same output?

Surely the answer would be: Both groups accurately preserved the original message in the first whisper. The same applies to *ḥadīth* chains when independent chains narrate the same report.

There are many other reasons as to why the analogy is a terrible one. These include that the message isn't being whispered, the participants are allowed to write the text, participants can ask their partners to repeat the message, the message is often available in public,[148] and perhaps most importantly, bad participants are removed from the game by being declared untrustworthy.

Objection 5: Shīʿa *Ḥadīths*

A Qur'ānist may object to *ḥadīths* by pointing out the existence of Shīʿa *ḥadīths*, which they will use to dismiss Sunnī *ḥadīths*, since surely, both corpuses cannot be correct.

The objection is understandable, but it is based upon flawed as-

148 *Ḥadīths* aren't usually heard by a narrator for the first time from the mouths of their teachers. In most cases, the narrations of scholars are circulated by others or are available with copyists. The student is merely going to the scholar to confirm the report and to have a shorter chain of narration to the Prophet ﷺ.

sumptions. Firstly, the number of authentic prophetic Shīʿa *ḥadīths* that conflict with authentic prophetic Sunnī *ḥadīths* is minimal, for most Shīʿa reports aren't from the Prophet ﷺ in the first place, but from his descendants. For instance, Jaʿfar bin Muḥammad (d. 148 AH) is the primary source of religious rulings in Shīʿism, not his great-great-great grandfather, the Prophet ﷺ. Unless Qur'ānists fully adhered to the opinions of Jaʿfar, determining whether his statements are correctly attributed to him or not shouldn't be a primary concern.

But yes, Sunnīs do have a major issue with the authenticity of Shīʿī reports due to multiple reasons. One of the main issues is the lack of variety of sources. For example, the vast majority of Shīʿa reports can be found in the works of three men, al-Kulaynī (d. 329 AH), al-Ṣadūq (d. 381 AH), and al-Ṭūsī (d. 460 AH). If any of these three narrators were to be considered unreliable, a Shīʿī is bound to lose trust in a large percentage of the Shīʿī corpus. For further reading on this topic, I would recommend my book *Distortions of al-Ṣadūq*, in which I've collected forty examples of clear manipulations by one of the three compilers.

Sunnīs, on the other hand, do not have this problem. Refer to my response to Objection 2.

Conclusion

The *isnād* system is a thorough system in which a narration is judged on multiple factors that mainly trace back to the reliability of the narrators and the connection of the report. An important point that needs to be appreciated is that even though the *isnād* system was created in order to preserve *ḥadīths*, the system was utilized by Muslims in other fields as well. History, *fiqh*, and even language, as we'll later see, all made use of the *isnād* system.

A Qur'ānist's biases against the *isnād* system are tied to their disillusionment with *ḥadīths*, but if asked about the system's utility for non-*ḥadīth* historical matters in general, a fair Qur'ānist wouldn't feel the urge to resist. After all, the system objectively trounces any other form of historical authentication.

In regards to *ḥadīths* specifically, we find many reports that include multiple corroborating chains, affirming the report's veracity. Scholars of *ḥadīth* take into consideration multiple intricate factors before judging a report as authentic.

- They examined the wording of reports in order to see whether or not there were any incorrect additions.
- They placed the students of major narrators into levels of accuracy in order to determine how to approach the reports of a teacher if there was a difference among the students.
- They compiled lists of students indicating whether they heard their teachers before or after a certain age at which their forgetfulness affected their reports.
- They called out narrators that attributed to their teachers that which they did not hear.

Hundreds of volumes were written with the intention of preserving the words of the Prophet ﷺ, and were successful in doing so, but they are left unappreciated by those that haven't delved into the science at all. It is a system exclusive to Islam, separating it from other histories, granting it the ability to ascertain truth from falsehood to the degree that even a word can be recognized as an addition.

Accessing the Qur'ān

The way in which the Qur'ānists speaks of the Qur'ān feels like it fell out of the heavens and onto their laps. Even though they take the Qur'ān for granted in its published form, by disconnecting themselves from Islamic history, they find themselves in multiple predicaments.

Our Recitation

Today, the vast majority of Muslims recite the Qur'ān according to the recitation of Ḥafṣ (d. 180 AH), while much of the North African population recites according to Warsh. However, in the 9th century AH, most Muslims were reciting the recitation of Abū 'Amr bin al-'Alā'.[149] Most, if not all translations of the Qur'ān today are based upon the Ḥafṣ recitation.

Most Qur'ānists seem to be unaware of the *qirā'āt* and it wouldn't be a surprise if they denied that they were actually reciting the Qur'ān according to the Ḥafṣ recitation. Some may even doubt the attribution, asking, "How do we know that a man named Ḥafṣ even read the Qur'ān in this manner?" Well, modern prints of the Qur'ān include his name in it. Furthermore, classical *qirā'āt* scholars, like Ibn Mujāhid (d. 324 AH) in his *al-Sab'a* and al-Dānī (d. 444 AH) in *Jāmi' al-Bayān*, listed out the variants among the recitations of the canonical reciters, and the mainstream recitation today matches the

149 Ibn al-Jazarī, *Ġāyat al-Nihāya*, 1/265.

recitation of Ḥafṣ.

These recitations have differences that are not confined to dialectal differences, but involve differences in meaning. The most famous example is Ḥafṣ' recitation of: "*Māliki yawm-iddīn* (**owner** of the Day of Judgment)," and Abū ʿAmr bin al-ʿAlā''s recitation of: "*Maliki yawm-iddīn* (**king** of the Day of Judgment)." (Q. 1:4).

The dominance of Ḥafṣ' recitation is very recent and the Qur'ānist needs to have a clear understanding of what the *qirā'āt* are in order to explain this reality. Is the Qur'ānist going to argue that all other recitations are false with the exception of the Ḥafṣ recitation? What about the vast majority of Muslims throughout history that did not adhere to Ḥafṣ? Does the existence of multiple different recitations mean that the Qur'ān is not preserved? By disconnecting themselves from centuries of the Islamic tradition, the Qur'ānist is blindly holding onto Ḥafṣ' recitation without justification. The people of the *sunnah* do have the answers though.

Firstly, Sunnīs believe that the Prophet ﷺ said, "The Qur'ān was revealed in seven modes." This report is narrated by at least eleven of his companions: ʿUmar,[150] ʿUthmān,[151] Ibn Masʿūd,[152] Abū Bakrah,[153] Ibn ʿAbbās,[154] Ḥuḏayfa,[155] Abū Hurayrah,[156] Abū Juhaym,[157] Umm

150 Al-Ṣanʿānī, *al-Muṣannaf*, 11/99.
151 Al-ʿAsqalānī, *al-Maṭālib al-ʿĀliya,* 8/121.
152 Ibn Abī Shayba, *al-Muṣannaf*, 6/138.
153 Ibn Ḥanbal, *Musnad Aḥmad*, p. 1455.
154 Ibn Sallām, *Faḍā'il al-Qur'ān*, p. 203.
155 Ibid., pp. 202-203.
156 Ibn Ḥibbān, *al-Iḥsān fī Taqrīb Ṣaḥīḥ Ibn Ḥibbān*, p. 309.
157 Al-Madanī, *Ḥādīth ʿAlī bin Ḥajar al-Saʿdī ʿan Ismāʿīl bin Jaʿfar al-*

Ayyūb,[158] Muʿād̲,[159] and Ubayy.[160] With this in mind, it shouldn't come to us as a surprise that some of the main reciters often recited in more than one mode. For example, al-Kisāʾī, one of the eponymous reciters, used to say, "I don't mind reading it as *maliki* or *māliki,*" (Q. 1:4) for both recitations are from Allah the Almighty.

The existence of the *qirāʾāt,* its manuals, the works explaining the variants, and the heritage surrounding them as a whole is what we expect to find because of the revelation of the Qurʾān in seven modes. This rich history is often ignored or denied by *ḥadīth* rejecters, because of their separation from Islamic history. In other words, they do not know why they recite what they recite.

The ʿUthmānic Codex

The scholars of Islam have always held the position that the Qurʾān may not be recited in a manner that conflicted with the ʿUthmānic Codex. Imām Mālik, in the second century, forbade the prayer behind one that recited according to the recitation of Ibn Masʿūd because it conflicted with the ʿUthmānic Codex.[161] Furthermore, Makkī (d. 437 AH) reported a consensus that it is not permissible to recite the Qurʾān in a manner that conflicts with the *muṣḥaf* of ʿUthmān.[162] This discussion doesn't only fail to show up among Qurʾān-only adherents, but the terms themselves are foreign to their

---

Madanī, pp. 378-379

158 Ibn Abī Shayba, *al-Muṣannaf*, 6/138.

159 Al-Ṭabarānī, *al-Muʿjam al-Kabīr*, 13/4676.

160 Al-Ṭayālisī, *Musnad Abī Dāwūd al-Ṭayālisī*, p. 94.

161 Al-Aṣbaḥī, *al-Mudawwana al-Kubrā*, 1/177.

162 Al-Qaysī, *al-Ibāna ʿan Maʿānī al-Qirāʾāt*, p. 192.

vocabulary.

These statements by classical scholars, plus much of the remnants of the *shāḏ* (anomalous) recitations found in *ḥadīth* and *tafsīr* literature, prove that some early Muslims at one point read the Qur'ān in a way that didn't fit in with the *muṣḥaf* that we have today.

But why are Muslims bound by 'Uthmān's codex?

The Qur'ānist is clueless as to the reasons, the history, the attribution of the codex to 'Uthmān, and would struggle to even argue for the preservation of the Qur'ān if confronted by a non-Muslim with questions about anomalous recitations.

Sunnīs, on the other hand, not only have the answers and acknowledge the history of 'Uthmān's codex, but embrace the narrative, instead of rejecting it.

In short, the reason for the codex was the differences between 'Irāqī and Shāmī reciters of the Qur'ān.[163] For the sake of unity, 'Uthmān limited the recitation to fit in with the Qurashī dialect.[164] Second generation Muslims like Ġunaym bin Qays (d. 90 AH) and Abū Mijlaz (d. 109 AH), professed that if 'Uthmān didn't write his codex, people would be reciting poetry instead,[165] implying that Muslims would be disillusioned by the disunity and would lack confidence in the Qur'ān. For further reading on the subject, refer to Dr. Azami's *The History of the Qur'ānic Text.*

While non-'Uthmānic recitations lasted for a while, mainly due to

163 Ibn Shabba, *Tārīkh al-Madīna*, 2/117.
164 Ibn Abī Dāwūd, *al-Maṣāḥif*, 1/214.
165 Ibid., 1/178.

Ibn Masʿūd's popularity in Kūfa, it didn't take too long before Muslim communities as a whole ultimately adopted the ʿUthmānic codex completely. Unfortunately, this discussion, as a whole, doesn't mean much to the Qur'ānist, who wouldn't even know how to attribute the agreed upon consonantal skeleton to ʿUthmān in the first place.

The Timing of the Revelations

The Qur'ān itself testifies that it wasn't revealed as a single revelation.

وَقَالَ الَّذِينَ كَفَرُوا لَوْلَا نُزِّلَ عَلَيْهِ الْقُرْآنُ جُمْلَةً وَاحِدَةً ۚ ﴿٣٢﴾

> And those who disbelieve say: "Why is not the Qur'ān revealed to him all at once?" (Q. 25:32)

Instead, it was revealed across a period of around twenty years. Since the Qur'ān was not compiled in order of revelation, we find verses that abrogate one another in ruling. In fact, we find example of scholars from the first century making the claim that the last chapter revealed was Sūrat al-Mā'idah, and that it doesn't contain any abrogated verses. These include ʿĀ'ishah (d. 58 AH), Abū Maysarah (d. 63 AH), al-Ḥasan (d. 110 AH), and ʿAṭiyyah bin Qays (d. 121 AH).[166]

With this in mind, the earliest Muslim exegetes, like Ibn ʿAbbās (d. 68 AH), ʿIkrimah (d. 105 AH), al-Ḥasan (d. 110 AH), Qatādah (d. 110 AH), and others provided lists of the chapters that were revealed in Makkah and Madīnah.[167] Based on these lists, if a ruling was found

---

166 Ibn Sallām, *Faḍā'il al-Qur'ān*, pp. 128-129.

167 Al-Suyūṭī, *al-Itqān fī ʿUlūm al-Qur'ān*, pp. 33-36. For example, al-Suyūṭī quotes al-Anbārī who provides his chain from Qatādah, who said: "The

in a Makkan verse that conflicts with a Madīnan verse, it would be understood that the Makkan ruling is abrogated.

Most Qur'ānists unreasonably reject the existence of the notion of abrogation and consequently run into trouble with verses that can only be explained as abrogating one another. A clear-cut example is the following:

يَا أَيُّهَا النَّبِيُّ حَرِّضِ الْمُؤْمِنِينَ عَلَى الْقِتَالِ ۚ إِن يَكُن مِّنكُمْ عِشْرُونَ صَابِرُونَ يَغْلِبُوا مِائَتَيْنِ ۚ وَإِن يَكُن مِّنكُم مِّائَةٌ يَغْلِبُوا أَلْفًا مِّنَ الَّذِينَ كَفَرُوا بِأَنَّهُمْ قَوْمٌ لَّا يَفْقَهُونَ ﴿٦٥﴾

Prophet, urge the believers to fight: if there are twenty of you who are steadfast, they will overcome two hundred, and a hundred of you, if steadfast, will overcome a thousand of the disbelievers, for they are people who do not understand.

الْآنَ خَفَّفَ اللَّهُ عَنكُمْ وَعَلِمَ أَنَّ فِيكُمْ ضَعْفًا ۚ فَإِن يَكُن مِّنكُم مِّائَةٌ صَابِرَةٌ يَغْلِبُوا مِائَتَيْنِ ۚ وَإِن يَكُن مِّنكُمْ أَلْفٌ يَغْلِبُوا أَلْفَيْنِ بِإِذْنِ اللَّهِ ۗ وَاللَّهُ مَعَ الصَّابِرِينَ ﴿٦٦﴾

---

following from the Qur'ān was revealed in Madīnah: *al-Baqara*, *Āl 'Imrān*, *al-Nisā'*, *al-Mā'ida*, *Barā'a*, *al-Ra'd*, *al-Naḥl*, *al-Ḥajj*, *al-Nūr*, *al-Aḥzāb*, *Muḥammad*, *al-Fatḥ*, *al-Ḥujurāt*, *al-Ḥadīd*, *al-Raḥmān*, *al-Mujādila*, *al-Ḥashr*, *al-Mumtaḥina*, *al-Ṣaff*, *al-Jumu'a*, *al-Munāfiqūn*, *al-Tagābun*, *al-Ṭalāq*, 'O' prophet why do you forbid' (Q. 66:1) to the tenth verse, 'When the earth is shaken' (Q. 99:1), 'When the victory of Allah has come' (Q. 110:1), while the rest is revealed in Makkah."

> **But God has lightened your burden for now**, knowing that there is weakness in you--a steadfast hundred of you will defeat two hundred and a steadfast thousand of you will defeat two thousand, by God's permission: God is with the steadfast. (Q. 8:65-66)

When verse 65 was revealed, the Muslims were ordered to fight even if they were outnumbered ten to one. This ruling was abrogated in verse 66, when the burden was lightened and they were only ordered to fight when they were outnumbered two to one. If the second verse was not revealed, the first order would've remained. This is a clear indication of the existence of abrogation of orders in the Qur'ān.

Even though the second verse succeeds the verse in compilation, they were obviously not revealed at the same time. This specific example is very useful for proving the concept of abrogation and doesn't require knowledge of Makkī and Madanī since the verses occur in succession.

An example of abrogation in which knowledge of Makkī and Madanī comes into play can be observed in the following:

وَإِنَّ لَكُمْ فِي الْأَنْعَامِ لَعِبْرَةً ۖ نُّسْقِيكُم مِّمَّا فِي بُطُونِهِ مِن بَيْنِ فَرْثٍ وَدَمٍ لَّبَنًا
خَالِصًا سَائِغًا لِّلشَّارِبِينَ ﴿٦٦﴾ وَمِن ثَمَرَاتِ النَّخِيلِ وَالْأَعْنَابِ تَتَّخِذُونَ مِنْهُ
سَكَرًا وَرِزْقًا حَسَنًا ۗ إِنَّ فِي ذَٰلِكَ لَآيَةً لِّقَوْمٍ يَعْقِلُونَ ﴿٦٧﴾

> And there is certainly a lesson for you in cattle: We give you to drink of what is in their bellies, from between digested food and blood: pure milk, pleasant to drink. And from the fruits of palm trees **and grapevines you derive intoxicants**

> **<u>as well as wholesome provision.</u>** Surely in this is a sign for those who understand. (Q. 16:66-67)

The Makkan verses above, list provisions from our Lord, implying the permissibility of intoxication. If no subsequent verses were revealed concerning alcohol, one wouldn't be able to make the argument that the Qur'ān prohibits intoxication. However, in Madīnah, the following was revealed:

يَا أَيُّهَا الَّذِينَ آمَنُوا لَا تَقْرَبُوا الصَّلَاةَ وَأَنتُمْ سُكَارَىٰ حَتَّىٰ تَعْلَمُوا مَا تَقُولُونَ وَلَا جُنُبًا إِلَّا عَابِرِي سَبِيلٍ حَتَّىٰ تَغْتَسِلُوا ۚ وَإِن كُنتُم مَّرْضَىٰ أَوْ عَلَىٰ سَفَرٍ أَوْ جَاءَ أَحَدٌ مِّنكُم مِّنَ الْغَائِطِ أَوْ لَامَسْتُمُ النِّسَاءَ فَلَمْ تَجِدُوا مَاءً فَتَيَمَّمُوا صَعِيدًا طَيِّبًا فَامْسَحُوا بِوُجُوهِكُمْ وَأَيْدِيكُمْ ۗ إِنَّ اللَّهَ كَانَ عَفُوًّا غَفُورًا ﴿٤٣﴾

> O believers! **<u>Do not approach prayer while intoxicated</u>** until you are aware of what you say, nor in a state of [full] impurity —unless you merely pass through [the mosque]— until you have bathed. But if you are ill, on a journey, or have relieved yourselves, or been intimate with your wives and cannot find water, then purify yourselves with clean earth, wiping your faces and hands. And Allah is Ever-Pardoning, All-Forgiving. (Q 4:43)

The verse above sets a specific limit. It allows intoxication but prohibits prayer during intoxication. Then, finally:

يَا أَيُّهَا الَّذِينَ آمَنُوا إِنَّمَا الْخَمْرُ وَالْمَيْسِرُ وَالْأَنصَابُ وَالْأَزْلَامُ رِجْسٌ مِّنْ عَمَلِ الشَّيْطَانِ فَاجْتَنِبُوهُ لَعَلَّكُمْ تُفْلِحُونَ ﴿٩٠﴾

> O believers! **Intoxicants,** gambling, idols, and drawing lots for decisions are all evil of Satan's handiwork. So shun them so you may be successful. (Q. 5:90)

This specific verse can be found in Sūrat al-Mā'idah, which is the revealed last chapter, according to multiple early authorities. Without knowledge of the timing of revelations, one could arguably push for an alternative understanding. A *ḥadīth*-rejecter may even argue that Q. 4:43 came after Q. 5:90, suggesting that alcohol can be consumed as long as that doesn't occur during prayer times, or that Q. 16:66-67 came after both verses and that intoxication is now permissible. The importance of the *sunnah* shines here as well, since the Prophet ﷺ punished those that consumed alcohol later in his life, as did the caliphs after him.[168]

One more example of two Madanī verses and the concept of abrogation revolves around leaving a will.

كُتِبَ عَلَيْكُمْ إِذَا حَضَرَ أَحَدَكُمُ الْمَوْتُ إِن تَرَكَ خَيْرًا الْوَصِيَّةُ لِلْوَالِدَيْنِ
وَالْأَقْرَبِينَ بِالْمَعْرُوفِ ۖ حَقًّا عَلَى الْمُتَّقِينَ ﴿١٨٠﴾

> It is prescribed that when death approaches any of you—if they leave something of value—**a will should be made in favor of parents** and immediate family with fairness. [This is] an obligation on those who are mindful [of Allah]. (Q. 2:180)

This verse, which explicitly instructs us to leave a will for our parents, is abrogated by the following verse in which the amount one leaves for their parents is specified:

168 Al-Nīsāpūrī, *Ṣaḥīḥ Muslim*, pp. 808-809.

يُوصِيكُمُ اللَّهُ فِي أَوْلَادِكُمْ ۖ لِلذَّكَرِ مِثْلُ حَظِّ الْأُنثَيَيْنِ ۚ فَإِن كُنَّ نِسَاءً
فَوْقَ اثْنَتَيْنِ فَلَهُنَّ ثُلُثَا مَا تَرَكَ ۖ وَإِن كَانَتْ وَاحِدَةً فَلَهَا النِّصْفُ ۚ وَلِأَبَوَيْهِ لِكُلِّ
وَاحِدٍ مِّنْهُمَا السُّدُسُ مِمَّا تَرَكَ إِن كَانَ لَهُ وَلَدٌ ۚ فَإِن لَّمْ يَكُن لَّهُ وَلَدٌ وَوَرِثَهُ
أَبَوَاهُ فَلِأُمِّهِ الثُّلُثُ ۚ فَإِن كَانَ لَهُ إِخْوَةٌ فَلِأُمِّهِ السُّدُسُ ۚ مِن بَعْدِ وَصِيَّةٍ يُوصِي
بِهَا أَوْ دَيْنٍ ۗ آبَاؤُكُمْ وَأَبْنَاؤُكُمْ لَا تَدْرُونَ أَيُّهُمْ أَقْرَبُ لَكُمْ نَفْعًا ۚ فَرِيضَةً
مِّنَ اللَّهِ ۗ إِنَّ اللَّهَ كَانَ عَلِيمًا حَكِيمًا ﴿١١﴾

> Allah commands you regarding your children: the share of the male will be twice that of the female. If you leave only two [or more] females, their share is two-thirds of the estate. But if there is only one female, her share will be one-half. **Each parent is entitled to one-sixth if you leave offspring. But if you are childless and your parents are the only heirs, then your mother will receive one-third. But if you leave siblings, then your mother will receive one-sixth—after the fulfilment of bequests and debts.** [Be fair to] your parents and children, as you do not [fully] know who is more beneficial to you. [This is] an obligation from Allah. Surely Allah is All-Knowing, All-Wise. (Q. 4:11)

If the latter verse wasn't revealed, the amounts chosen to be left for parents would have been optional. This flexibility ended with the revelation of Q. 4:11.

Conclusion

The Qur'ānist is ignorant about Qur'ānic sciences. Describing this as ironic is an understatement. Qur'ānic sciences are necessary since without them we can't access the Qur'ān. By merely examining aspects that Qur'ānists have taken for granted, like the recitation, the 'Uthmānic codex, and the timing of the revelations, we can see that their adherence to the Qur'ān is based upon blind faith through imitating the people of the *sunnah* who have a monopoly on these sciences.

Understanding the Qur'ān through *Ḥadīth*

During discussions with Qur'ānists, one often finds them claiming that they are not interested in anyone's understanding except their own. The Qur'ān-only approach is individualistic, placing one's intellect and ability to access the knowledge of the Qur'ān above all else. The people of the *sunnah*, on the other hand, hold onto classical scholarship, due to their knowledge of the context of the verses and the language.

After all, how can a contemporary student of the Qur'ān be placed on the same level as Ibn Masʿūd, the companion of the Prophet ﷺ? How can anyone equal he who said, "There is not a chapter in the book of Allah that I'm not aware of where it was revealed nor a verse that I am not aware what it was revealed about."[169] Can a Qur'ānist even dare to say something similar?!

The Clarity of the Qur'ān

The Qur'ān is clear... but who is it clear to? The Qur'ān is clear to the seventh century Arab, yes. It is not clear to those that have not studied the language. A translation of the Qur'ān may be clear to the non-Arab. However, a translation of the Qur'ān is not the Qur'ān. Much of the Qur'ān is clear to the average contemporary Arab, but the Qur'ān contains classical vocabulary that is not used in colloquial speech. Hence, even the modern Arab often has to return to

169 Al-Nīsāpūrī, *Ṣaḥīḥ Muslim*, p. 1133.

classical works of exegesis in order to better understand the Qur'ān. The classical works often include explanations by the Companions of the Prophet ﷺ and their students, often defining difficult terms. We also often find definitions derived from pre-Islamic poetry in order to give validity to a particular definition.

A practical example can be demonstrated with the term *ḥamīm* (Q. 6:70, 37: 67, 38:57, 56:93). Returning to Lane's Lexicon will provide us with multiple results including the following:

> Cold water: (Ḳ:) or *cold*, applied to water: so, accord. to IAạr, in the saying of a poet,
>
> وَسَاغَ لِيَ الشَّرَابُ وَكُنْتُ قِدمًا   أَكَادُ أَغَصُّ بِالمَاءِ الحَمِيْمِ
>
> [And wine has become easy to swallow to me, whereas I used, in old time, nearly to be choked with cold water]: (Az, TA)[170]

By returning to Lane's source, al-Azharī's (d. 370 AH) *Tahḏīb*, we find this line of poetry preceded by Abū al-ʿAbbās Thaʿlab (d. 291 AH) asking Ibn al-Aʿrābī (d. 231 AH) the definition of the term *ḥamīm,* in which he responds by quoting al-Nābiġa al-Ḏibyānī's (d. 18 BH) poem.[171] We can conclude that the term was not commonly used and that a great scholar of language had to produce an example from pre-Islamic poetry to support his chosen definition. Classical lexicons and works of *tafsīr* are filled with similar examples, in which classical poetry is used to define an unfamiliar term found in the Qur'ān.

170 Lane, *An Arabic–English Lexicon*, 1/637.
171 Al-Azharī, *Muʿjam Tahḏīb al-Luġa*, 1/929.

At times, a definition will make its way into a lexicon merely because it was used in a particular manner by a Bedouin when reciting a line of poetry, despite uncertainty regarding its validity. For example, al-Farā' said, "I heard some Arabs use the term *mā'ūn* to mean 'water.'"[172] Unfortunately, some of that poetry is forged, like the usage of the term *juz'* to refer to females. Al-Azharī commented, "I did not find this in the old poetry or in what was reported from trustworthy Arabs, and one should pay no heed to that line, for it is a forgery."[173]

To make things a little more complicated, sometimes, a classical scholar will attribute a meaning to a term using an *isnād* to an earlier linguist. Abū Bakr al-Sijistāni quotes Abū 'Umar, from Tha'lab, from 'Alī bin Ṣāliḥ, that al-Kisā'ī said that some Arabs say, "*'Āla / ya'ūlu* (Q. 4:3) is used if one has a lot of children." He also quotes Abū 'Abdillāh, who narrated from Abū 'Umar, from al-Hudhud, from al-Mubarrid that "*al-'Anat* (Q. 4:25) according to Arabs is to give one a burden that they cannot bear."[174]

The purpose of bringing forth these examples is to show that accessing the Qur'ān isn't as simple as opening up a lexicon in order to extract a definition. The *isnād* system that Qur'ānists shy away from is integrated into our classical dictionaries that documented the language. Lines of poetry, often attributed to a random Bedouin, result in the creation of additional entries under a word. A verse that was clear to a first century Arab is not clear to a contemporary Arab, let alone a non-Arab who has to rely on Lane's Lexicon, that is quoting

172 Al-Sijistānī, *Nuzhat al-Qulūb fī Tafsīr Ġarīb al-Qur'ān al-'Azīz*, p. 416-417.
173 Al-Azharī, *Mu'jam Tahḏīb al-Luġa*, 1/595.
174 Al-Sijistānī, *Nuzhat al-Qulūb fī Tafsīr Ġarīb al-Qur'ān al-'Azīz*, pp. 196, 324.

a classical linguist, who is quoting an unknown poet for the meaning of a word. Fortunately, lexicons do make use of the first generations of Muslims in order to explain much of the Qur'ān, in the same way that classical works of *tafsīr* do. For example, al-Azharī used Ibn 'Abbās, the Prophet's ﷺ cousin, to define *sāmidūn, al-ḥaraj, al-'adl, mu'ṣirāt.*[175] Classical lexicographers benefited from authorities, like Mujāhid and Qatādah, when it came to understanding the language of the Qur'ān. Of course, these men were prolific *ḥadīth* narrators as well who were often used to understand the context of many verses, as we'll soon see.

The Historical Context of the Qur'ān

While much of the Qur'ān is addressing the first generation of Muslims, there was a time in which there was no Muslim community. The whole body of Muslims was made up of a few individuals. Much of what was revealed in Makkah was directed towards the polytheists of Quraysh, which, as an audience, cannot be any more different than the modern Muslim audience that the Qur'ān speaks to today. A text will hold different meanings to different audiences, and the Qur'ān is not an exception to that rule.

The Qur'ānist will argue that the Qur'ān is timeless, suitable for all environments, and thus they have the ability to understand it in the same way the first audience did. Nobody is disputing the timelessness of the Qur'ān. Benefit can be obtained from a message, even if it was initially connected to a specific incident. Though, at times, as we'll soon see, stripping the Qur'ān away from its historical context takes away layers of meaning from the text.

175 Al-Azharī, *Mu'jam Tahḏīb al-Luġa*, 1/775.

The historical context of the Qur'ān, the traditions of pre-Islamic Arabs, and the events surrounding the life of the Prophet ﷺ and his Companions, are intertwined with many Qur'ānic verses. Unfortunately, these Qur'ānic verses cannot mean much to those that shun the *sunnah* and below are a few examples surrounding one aspect of Islam, the pilgrimage, which demonstrate that reality.

يَسْأَلُونَكَ عَنِ الْأَهِلَّةِ ۖ قُلْ هِيَ مَوَاقِيتُ لِلنَّاسِ وَالْحَجِّ ۗ وَلَيْسَ الْبِرُّ بِأَن تَأْتُوا
الْبُيُوتَ مِن ظُهُورِهَا وَلَٰكِنَّ الْبِرَّ مَنِ اتَّقَىٰ ۗ وَأْتُوا الْبُيُوتَ مِنْ أَبْوَابِهَا ۚ وَاتَّقُوا
اللَّهَ لَعَلَّكُمْ تُفْلِحُونَ ﴿١٨٩﴾

> They ask you about the crescent moons. Say, "They are measurements of time for the people and for *ḥajj*." **<u>And it is not righteousness to enter houses from the back</u>**, but righteousness is one who fears Allah. And enter houses from their doors. And fear Allah that you may succeed. (Q. 2:189)

Without returning to exegetical works, what would you assume that this verse was referring to? Is this about the mannerisms of entering one's own home? Or is this about how one should approach the homes of others? The answer is: Neither.

The companion of the Prophet ﷺ, Al-Barā' bin 'Āzib (d. 72 AH), explains that "If the Anṣār went off to the pilgrimage, they would not enter from their doors, but they would enter from the back, so Allah the Almighty revealed, 'It is not righteousness to enter houses from the back.'"[176]

176 Al-Nasā'ī, *al-Sunan al-Kubrā*, 3/1727.

The next report on the same page provides more details. Al-Barā' elaborates, "The people of pre-Islamic times, when in a state of *iḥrām*, did not enter their houses from the doors, but would enter from the back, through the walls."

Al-Zuhrī (d. 124 AH) adds that the Anṣār that set out for Makkah did not let anything get in between them and the sky, as a form of humility. If one of them realized that they forgot something at home "he would return but without entering the door, due to the roof that would get in between him and the sky, so he would open the wall from behind."[177]

The contemporary Muslim would have no idea of these pre-Islamic superstitions or rituals, and they wouldn't be able to extract these ideas from the verse. Instead, they would probably assume that the verses were reprimanding those that snooped around the houses of others or that it was teaching some etiquette. One wouldn't be able to understand how this order is connected to the mentioning of the pilgrimage in the verse unless they were familiar with the historical context provided in *ḥadīth* literature.

There are other verses that are related to the pilgrimage that also require a deeper understanding of that era, for instance:

إِنَّ الصَّفَا وَالْمَرْوَةَ مِن شَعَائِرِ اللَّهِ ۖ فَمَنْ حَجَّ الْبَيْتَ أَوِ اعْتَمَرَ فَلَا جُنَاحَ
عَلَيْهِ أَن يَطَّوَّفَ بِهِمَا ۚ وَمَن تَطَوَّعَ خَيْرًا فَإِنَّ اللَّهَ شَاكِرٌ عَلِيمٌ ﴿١٥٨﴾

Indeed, aṣ-Ṣafā and al-Marwah are among the symbols of Allah. So whoever makes *ḥajj* to the House or performs *'umrah*

177 Al-Ṭabarī, *Tafsīr al-Ṭabarī*, 2/193.

> - there is no blame upon him for walking between them. And whoever volunteers good - then indeed, Allah is Appreciative and Knowing. (Q. 2:158)

The following conversation occurs between 'Ā'ishah and her nephew 'Urwah. He said, "'Indeed, aṣ-Ṣafā and al-Marwah are among the symbols of Allah. So, whoever makes *ḥajj* to the House or performs *'umrah* - there is no blame upon him for walking between them,' so there is no issue if he did not walk between them." 'Ā'ishah responded by saying, "No. If it was what you said, it would've been: There is no blame upon him for **not** walking between them." She then explained that the Anṣār used to worship the idol Manāt and avoided al-Ṣafā and al-Marwah, but when they became Muslims, they asked about it, and thus, the verse was revealed.[178]

Notice how 'Urwah, a second generation Muslim who was young at the time, misunderstood a verse, because he wasn't aware of the context of the revelation. Of course, we are in a worse position today.

Another verse that is tied to pilgrimage is the following:

> ثُمَّ أَفِيضُوا مِنْ حَيْثُ أَفَاضَ النَّاسُ وَاسْتَغْفِرُوا اللَّهَ ۚ إِنَّ اللَّهَ غَفُورٌ رَّحِيمٌ ﴿١٩٩﴾
>
> Then depart from the place from where the people depart and ask forgiveness of Allah. Indeed, Allah is Forgiving and Merciful. (Q. 2:199)

The Qur'ān provides an order to depart from a specific place, which it simply refers to as "where the people depart" from. This could be understood as 'Arafah which is mentioned in the previous verse in

178 Al-Aṣbaḥī, *al-Muwaṭṭá*, pp. 208-209.

the chapter or could be referring to another place altogether, like al-Muzdalifah, since historically, Quraysh departed from Muzdalifah, not ʿArafah. Furthermore, what is the significance of the words "the people?" Why doesn't the verse simply say, "Then depart and ask forgiveness?"

ʿĀʾishah explains, "Quraysh and those that held its beliefs would stand at al-Muzdalifah and they would be referred to as "al-Ḥums," while the rest of the Arabs would stand at ʿArafah. So when Islam came, Allah the Almighty ordered His prophet ﷺ to go to ʿArafah, stand upon it, then depart from it, and that is what is meant by, 'Then depart from where the people depart.'" In the next *ḥadīth* in the same chapter, ʿĀʾishah says, "The Ḥums would not leave al-Muzdalifah, while all the people would go up to ʿArafah."[179]

Qurʾānists that do perform the pilgrimage ultimately perform it in the same way that other Muslims do. However, this is due to their imitation of the masses in their understanding of the Qurʾān and *sunnah*. Furthermore, the verse not only provides pilgrimage instructions, but ends the separation between the Ḥums and other Arabs. In that way, it is similar to the following verse:

يَا بَنِي آدَمَ خُذُوا زِينَتَكُمْ عِندَ كُلِّ مَسْجِدٍ وَكُلُوا وَاشْرَبُوا وَلَا تُسْرِفُوا ۚ إِنَّهُ لَا يُحِبُّ الْمُسْرِفِينَ ﴿٣١﴾

> O children of ʾĀdam, **take on your adornment at every mosque**. Eat and drink and do not be extravagant. Surely, He does not like the extravagant. (Q. 7:31)

---

179 Al-Nīsāpūrī, *Ṣaḥīḥ Muslim*, p. 559.

Al-Zuhrī provides us with the historical context:

> The Arabs used to circumambulate the House (of Allah) while in the nude, except for al-Ḥums and their allies. As for the others, they would leave their clothes and circumambulate in the clothes of al-Ḥums, for it was allowed to wear their clothes. If they didn't find someone to lend them from among al-Ḥums, then they would leave their clothes and circumambulate in the nude. If they did circumambulate with their own clothes, then they would leave it after circumambulating, forbidding it upon themselves, and that is why Allah the Almighty said, "Take on your adornment at every mosque."[180]

Ibn ʿAbbās, furthermore, ties the revelation of the verse to a woman that was only able to conceal her private parts.[181] This understanding wouldn't have been derived by a Qur'ānist who would perhaps assume that the verse is specifically about dressing nicely when going to the mosque. By doing this, they would also be ignoring the very next verse:

قُلْ مَنْ حَرَّمَ زِينَةَ اللَّهِ الَّتِي أَخْرَجَ لِعِبَادِهِ وَالطَّيِّبَاتِ مِنَ الرِّزْقِ ۚ قُلْ هِيَ لِلَّذِينَ آمَنُوا فِي الْحَيَاةِ الدُّنْيَا خَالِصَةً يَوْمَ الْقِيَامَةِ ۗ كَذَٰلِكَ نُفَصِّلُ الْآيَاتِ لِقَوْمٍ يَعْلَمُونَ ﴿٣٢﴾

> Say, "**Who has prohibited the adornment Allah has brought forth for His servants**, and the wholesome things of sustenance?" Say, "They are for the believers during this

180 Al-Ṣanʿānī, *Tafsīr Abd al-Razzāq*, 3/77.
181 Al-Nīsāpūrī, *Ṣaḥīḥ Muslim*, pp. 1354-1355.

worldly life (though shared by others), while they are purely for them on the day of Resurrection. This is how We elaborate the verses for people who understand." (Q. 71:32)

The verse is rebuking those that prohibited wearing clothes, linking it to the acts of Satan a few verses earlier.

يَا بَنِي آدَمَ لَا يَفْتِنَنَّكُمُ الشَّيْطَانُ كَمَا أَخْرَجَ أَبَوَيْكُم مِّنَ الْجَنَّةِ يَنزِعُ عَنْهُمَا لِبَاسَهُمَا لِيُرِيَهُمَا سَوْآتِهِمَا ۗ إِنَّهُ يَرَاكُمْ هُوَ وَقَبِيلُهُ مِنْ حَيْثُ لَا تَرَوْنَهُمْ ۗ إِنَّا جَعَلْنَا الشَّيَاطِينَ أَوْلِيَاءَ لِلَّذِينَ لَا يُؤْمِنُونَ ﴿٢٧﴾

O children of 'Ādam, "Do not let Satan put you in trouble the way he had your parents expelled from Paradise, **having their dress removed from them, so that he could show them their shame**. Indeed, he sees you - he and his company - from where you do not see them. Surely, We have made the devils friends to those who do not believe. (Q. 7:27)

However, this connection is one that cannot be made without being aware of the action of the Ḥums and their oppression against other Arabs.

Even though the Qur'ān is for all mankind, it was initially revealed to a specific audience. An audience that was familiar with the language, rituals, and environment. When the Qur'ān speaks of a well-known matter, it doesn't need to provide details to its audience. Another example of this occurs in the following verse:

الْحَجُّ أَشْهُرٌ مَّعْلُومَاتٌ ۚ فَمَن فَرَضَ فِيهِنَّ الْحَجَّ فَلَا رَفَثَ وَلَا فُسُوقَ وَلَا

جِدَالَ فِي الْحَجِّ ۗ وَمَا تَفْعَلُوا مِنْ خَيْرٍ يَعْلَمْهُ اللَّهُ ۗ وَتَزَوَّدُوا فَإِنَّ خَيْرَ الزَّادِ
التَّقْوَىٰ ۚ وَاتَّقُونِ يَا أُولِي الْأَلْبَابِ ﴿١٩٧﴾

Ḥajj is during well-known months, so whoever has made *ḥajj* obligatory upon himself therein, there is no sexual relations and no disobedience and no disputing during *ḥajj*. And whatever good you do - Allah knows it. And take provisions, but indeed, the best provision is fear of Allah. And fear Me, O you of understanding. (Q. 2:197)

But what are the well-known months? What used to be seen as well-known no longer is. The average Muslim, if asked this question, wouldn't be able to list the months that the verse is referring to. Fortunately for contemporary Muslims, the Companions of the Prophet ﷺ, like Ibn Masʿūd, Ibn ʿUmar, and Ibn ʿAbbās, stated that these are referring to Shawwāl, Ḏū al-Qiʿdah, and Ḏū al-Ḥijjah.[182]

These months should not be confused with the four that are mentioned in Sūrat al-Tawbah:

إِنَّ عِدَّةَ الشُّهُورِ عِندَ اللَّهِ اثْنَا عَشَرَ شَهْرًا فِي كِتَابِ اللَّهِ يَوْمَ خَلَقَ السَّمَاوَاتِ
وَالْأَرْضَ مِنْهَا أَرْبَعَةٌ حُرُمٌ ۚ ذَٰلِكَ الدِّينُ الْقَيِّمُ ۚ فَلَا تَظْلِمُوا فِيهِنَّ أَنفُسَكُمْ ۚ
وَقَاتِلُوا الْمُشْرِكِينَ كَافَّةً كَمَا يُقَاتِلُونَكُمْ كَافَّةً ۚ وَاعْلَمُوا أَنَّ اللَّهَ مَعَ الْمُتَّقِينَ
﴿٣٦﴾

Indeed, the number of months with Allah is twelve months in the register of Allah from the day He created the heavens and

182 Al-Ṭabarī, *Tafsīr al-Ṭabarī*, 2/267-268.

the earth; of these, **four are ḥurum (sacred)**. That is the correct religion, so do not wrong yourselves during them. And fight against the disbelievers collectively as they fight against you collectively. And know that Allah is with the righteous. (Q. 9:36)

Muḥarram, the first month in the year, should be quite an obvious pick, due its name, but what about the other months? The Prophet ﷺ explains in a *ḥadīth* that these are D̲ū al-Qiʿda, D̲ū al-Ḥijjah, Muḥarram, and Rajab.[183]

By merely examining a few verses of the Qur'ān that pertain to the pilgrimage, we've come across multiple instances of the text that would be left misunderstood and unappreciated without the historical context. It should not come as a surprise that the first audience of the Qur'ān understood it in a manner that surpasses ours simply due to being of that environment.

Ponder upon these verses:

أَفَرَأَيْتُمُ اللَّاتَ وَالْعُزَّىٰ ﴿١٩﴾ وَمَنَاةَ الثَّالِثَةَ الْأُخْرَىٰ ﴿٢٠﴾ أَلَكُمُ الذَّكَرُ وَلَهُ الْأُنثَىٰ
﴿٢١﴾ تِلْكَ إِذًا قِسْمَةٌ ضِيزَىٰ ﴿٢٢﴾ إِنْ هِيَ إِلَّا أَسْمَاءٌ سَمَّيْتُمُوهَا أَنتُمْ وَآبَاؤُكُم مَّا
أَنزَلَ اللَّهُ بِهَا مِن سُلْطَانٍ ۚ إِن يَتَّبِعُونَ إِلَّا الظَّنَّ وَمَا تَهْوَى الْأَنفُسُ ۖ وَلَقَدْ
جَاءَهُم مِّن رَّبِّهِمُ الْهُدَىٰ ﴿٢٣﴾

So have you considered al-Lāt and al-ʿUzzā? And Manāt, the third - the other one? Is the male for you and for Him the female? That, then, is an unjust division. They are not but

183 Al-Sijistānī, *Sunan Abī Dāwūd,* p. 284.

> names you have named them - you and your forefathers - for which Allah has sent down no authority. They follow not except assumption and what souls desire, and there has already come to them from their Lord guidance. (Q. 53:19-23)

These idols don't mean much to anyone from our generation since they were destroyed a thousand four hundred years ago. However, to the first audience of the Qur'ān, these are verses that condemned the worship of their idols. The impact of the verses upon both groups is incomparable.

While it is surely impossible to fully place ourselves in the shoes of a first century Arab, we do have access to information about their lives, practices, and beliefs. Merely by studying the previous verses, we're able to extract that information and appreciate the Qur'ān on another level, which unfortunately the *ḥadīth*-rejecter simply cannot.

Is Qur'ān-only Islam Easier?

The *ḥadīth*-rejection position is reactionary. One comes across a *ḥadīth* they dislike and they stomach it. They come across another and roll with it. Then one day, they think to themselves: "Why should I bother following all these *ḥadīths* that I don't like? I'll just stick with the Qur'ān."

They have forgotten that Allah the Almighty said:

فَلَا وَرَبِّكَ لَا يُؤْمِنُونَ حَتَّىٰ يُحَكِّمُوكَ فِيمَا شَجَرَ بَيْنَهُمْ ثُمَّ لَا يَجِدُوا فِي
أَنفُسِهِمْ حَرَجًا مِّمَّا قَضَيْتَ وَيُسَلِّمُوا تَسْلِيمًا ﴿٦٥﴾

> But no, by your Lord, they will never attain faith until they make you judge in their disputes, then find within themselves no discomfort from whatever you have decreed and submit completely. (Q. 4:65)

This verse clearly tells us that we have to submit to matters that we dislike. Surely, if everything in Islam was to our liking, then where would the test be?

Unfortunately, Qurʾānists are often affected by the values of Western liberalism, which leads many of them to understand the Qurʾān in a way that conflicts with the traditional understanding. This causes them to give their own individual interpretations precedence over the intention of the Creator. Observe the following verse:

وَالسَّارِقُ وَالسَّارِقَةُ فَاقْطَعُوا أَيْدِيَهُمَا جَزَاءً بِمَا كَسَبَا نَكَالًا مِّنَ اللَّهِ ۗ وَاللَّهُ عَزِيزٌ حَكِيمٌ ﴿٣٨﴾

> As for male and female thieves, *faqṭaʿū aydiyahuma* for what they have done—a deterrent from Allah. And Allah is Almighty, All-Wise. (Q. 5:38)

Some Qurʾānists argue that the terms "*faqṭaʿū aydiyahuma*" is a metaphor for anything but the literal "cut off their hands." Surprisingly, those that hold this view would rather have you believe that the Author of the Qurʾān is an ineffective communicator, as long as the text lines in with their values. The phrasing of "*faqtaʿū aydiyahuma*" is the most appropriate choice of words if one were to order the cutting off of the hands. The effects of this intentional word choice led to many people losing their hands throughout the centuries. Couldn't Allah, in His infinite wisdom, choose some other words to communicate His intent?

Not surprisingly, the early scholars of Islam all understood the verse literally, including Abū Bakr, ʿUmar, ʿUthmān, ʿAlī, ʿĀʾishah, al-Zubayr, ʿAmmar, Ibn ʿAbbās, Ibn Masʿūd, Abū Hurayrah, Abū Saʿīd, Anas, Ibn al-Zubayr, ʿAbdullāh bin ʿAmr bin al-ʿĀṣ, al-Shaʿbī, Saʿīd bin Jubayr, ʿAtāʾ, Makḥūl, Ṭāwūs, Abū Jaʿfar, ʿUmar bin ʿAbd al-ʿAzīz, Abū al-Aswad, and others.[184]

In any case, if one were to take the verse literally, the Qurʾān would be harsher than if we were to apply *ḥadīths*, since the Prophet ﷺ used to only cut off the hand of one who stole something that was equivalent to the price of a shield.[185] ʿUrwah explains that "the thief would lose his hand during the time of the Prophet ﷺ if he stole what equated to the price of a shield, which was (relatively) expensive at the time, and it would not be cut over a trivial thing."[186]

To summarize, if one were to steal a loaf of bread, they would lose their hand if the authorities were literalist Qurʾānists, but they would be spared if the authorities followed the *sunnah*.

Another verse that the Qurʾānist may find problematic would be the following:

وَيَسْأَلُونَكَ عَنِ الْمَحِيضِ ۖ قُلْ هُوَ أَذًى فَاعْتَزِلُوا النِّسَاءَ فِي الْمَحِيضِ ۖ وَلَا
تَقْرَبُوهُنَّ حَتَّىٰ يَطْهُرْنَ ۖ فَإِذَا تَطَهَّرْنَ فَأْتُوهُنَّ مِنْ حَيْثُ أَمَرَكُمُ اللَّهُ ۚ إِنَّ اللَّهَ

184 Ibn Abī Shayba, *al-Muṣannaf*, 5/470-474.
185 Al-Nīsāpūrī, *Ṣaḥīḥ Muslim*, p. 799.
186 Ibn Abī Shayba, *al-Muṣannaf*, 5/473.

يُحِبُّ ٱلتَّوَّٰبِينَ وَيُحِبُّ ٱلْمُتَطَهِّرِينَ ﴿٢٢٢﴾

> And they ask you about menstruation. Say, "It is harm, **so keep away from wives during menstruation.** And do not approach them until they are pure. And when they have purified themselves, then come to them from where Allah has ordained for you. Indeed, Allah loves those who are constantly repentant and loves those who purify themselves." (Q. 2:222)

If Qur'ānists were to take the verse literally, it would mean that one should not approach their wives at all during her period in the same way that the Jews of Madīnah did in accordance to the Old Testament.[187] Fortunately, the *sunnah* clarifies that this verse is referring to intercourse specifically and the Prophet ﷺ explicitly states, "Do whatever you wish except for intercourse."[188]

Does the Qur'ānist have the liberty to make that interpretation though? Or is the Qur'ān subject to the whims and desires of the reader? How would a Qur'ānist approach a verse like the one below without context?

---

187 Leviticus 15:19-31: "When a woman has a discharge, and the discharge in her body is blood, she shall be in her menstrual impurity for seven days, and whoever touches her shall be unclean until the evening. And everything on which she lies during her menstrual impurity shall be unclean. Everything also on which she sits shall be unclean. And whoever touches her bed shall wash his clothes and bathe himself in water and be unclean until the evening. And whoever touches anything on which she sits shall wash his clothes and bathe himself in water and be unclean until the evening... Thus you shall keep the people of Israel separate from their uncleanness, lest they die in their uncleanliness by defiling my tabernacle that is in their midst."

188 Al-Nīsāpūrī, *Ṣaḥīḥ Muslim*, p. 179.

يَا أَيُّهَا الَّذِينَ آمَنُوا كُتِبَ عَلَيْكُمُ الْقِصَاصُ فِي الْقَتْلَى ۖ الْحُرُّ بِالْحُرِّ وَالْعَبْدُ
بِالْعَبْدِ وَالْأُنثَىٰ بِالْأُنثَىٰ ﴿١٧٨﴾

> O' believers! [The law of] retaliation is set for you in cases of murder—a free man for a free man, a slave for a slave, and a female for a female. (Q. 2: 178)

Would a Qur'ānist assume that a free man can have another free man take his place instead? Wouldn't that be the default way one would understand the verse? The purpose of the verse is completely lost upon those that are not familiar with the historical context behind the verse.

Qatādah (d. 110 AH) explains, "The people of pre-Islamic times were a people of oppression and adherence to the Shayṭān. If a group from among them with number and strength had their slave killed by a slave of another group, they would say, 'We will not kill but a free man in return,' due to their pride in their superiority. If one of their women was killed by a woman, they would say, 'We will not kill but a man in return.' So then Allah revealed this verse, 'A free man for a free man, a slave for a slave, and a female for a female,' prohibiting them from this oppression."[189]

The solution, once again, comes from the context provided by a first century scholar, demonstrating what sort of chaos could ensue if we approached the Qur'ān without returning to the historical context.

189 Al-Marwazī, *Ta'ẓīm Qadr al-Ṣalāt* ,p. 366.

Conclusion

There is no doubt that much of the Qur'ān does not require an explanation, but there is a major difference between the understanding of a layperson and a scholar. Much of the Qur'ān was made easy and accessible to everyone. However, there are layers of depth that cannot be accessed by those that disconnect themselves from the tradition.

وَأَنَّهُۥ هُوَ رَبُّ ٱلشِّعْرَىٰ ﴿٤٩﴾

And He alone is the Lord of Sirius. (Q. 53:49)

What does this verse mean to those that don't know of the tradition? Isn't Allah the Almighty the Lord of all things, so why is He specifically the Lord of Sirius? To the Arabs at the time, this verse was rebuking the tribes that worshipped Sirius.[190]

Every phrase in the Qur'ān, every word, has a purpose, and we are at a major disadvantage. We are disconnected from the environment of the Qur'ān in time. Unfortunately, those are the cards that we were dealt and there is no perfect solution. We do have a choice to make though. We can either choose to make use of the remnants of the context of that environment by embracing it or we may choose to reject it.

190 Al-Ṭabarī, *Tafsīr al-Ṭabarī*, 11/537.

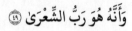

Prophecy on *Ḥadīth* Rejection

No text on the importance of *ḥadīth* can be complete without mentioning the famous report that foreshadows the emergence of the Qur'ānist movement. The *ḥadīth* is reported by multiple companions of the Prophet ﷺ in tens of *ḥadīth* compilations and is authentic through the paths of al-Miqdām bin Maʿdī Karib, Abū Rāfiʿ, and al-ʿIrbāḍ bin Sāriya.

The Narration of al-Miqdām

ʿAbd al-Raḥmān bin Abī ʿAwf reports that al-Miqdām narrated that the Prophet ﷺ said: "Verily, I have been sent the Qur'ān and something like it. Verily, I have been sent the Qur'ān and something like it. Verily, a man whose stomach is full while on his couch shall say: Refer to the Qur'ān and what you find within it as permissible, then make it permissible, and what you find within it impermissible, then make it impermissible..."

The narration of al-Miqdām bin Maʿdī Karib comes through two of his students ʿAbd al-Raḥmān bin Abī ʿAwf the judge of Ḥimṣ,[191] as well as al-Ḥasan bin Jābir.[192] It was also narrated by his son Yaḥyā bin al-Miqdām, who narrated to his son, Ṣāliḥ bin Yaḥyā bin al-

---

191 Al-Ashyab, *Juz' al-Ḥasan bin Mūsā al-Ashyab,* p. 73; Al-Tarqufī, *Juz' al-Tarqufī*, p. 108.
192 Al-Dārimī, *Musnad al-Dārimī*, 1/96.

Miqdām. Al-Ṭabarānī provides two chains to Ṣāliḥ,[193] both of which are weak, but it is unlikely that both paths are fabricated since there is no clear motive to attribute this narration to Ṣāliḥ, especially since the report to al-Miqdām has already been established through valid chains. Al-Ṭabarānī's reports include a strange addition in which al-Miqdām is narrating from Khālid bin al-Walīd, which conflicts with the authentic paths, and thus should be rejected. The report is a Shāmī narration.

The Narration of Abū Rāfiʿ

Abū Rāfiʿ narrated that the Prophet ﷺ said: "Let me not find one of you on his couch in which if he was approached by an order that I gave or prohibited he'd say: I don't know! We only follow what we find in the book of Allah."

The narration of Abū Rāfiʿ is a Madanī report and is narrated by Ibn ʿUyaynah who mentioned two paths. The first is a connected report from Sālim from the son of Abū Rāfiʿ, while the second is from Ibn al-Munkadir who narrates it without a chain to the Prophet ﷺ,[194] establishing that this report was available to second generation Muslims. Ibn ʿUyaynah's report from Sālim is corroborated by Mālik.[195]

The Narration of al-ʿIrbāḍ

Al-ʿIrbāḍ narrated that the Prophet ﷺ said: "Does one of you think that while he is resting on his couch that Allah only forbade what

193 Al-Ṭabarānī, *al-Muʿjam al-Kabīr*, 3/959.
194 Sanjar, *Musnad al-Shāfiʿī*, 4/63.
195 Ibn Ḥibbān, *al-Iḥsān fī Taqrīb Ṣaḥīḥ Ibn Ḥibbān*, p. 112.

is in the Qur'ān? By Allah, I have preached, ordered, and forbade matters that are like the Qur'ān or more (in number)."

The path of al-ʿIrbāḍ bin Sāriya,[196] like al-Miqdām's, is Shāmī as well. The report is a useful corroboration to the two previous established reports even though it is solely reported by Ashaʿth bin Shuʿba who has been weakened by Abū Zurʿah.[197] Fortunately, there is validity in the opinion supporting his trustworthiness, for he has been deemed as such by Abū Dāwūd[198] and al-Ṭabarānī.[199]

By combining the chains of the reports above, excluding repetitive chains that don't add much to the overall picture, it is very hard to deny the attribution of this narration to the Prophet ﷺ. Keep in mind the divergence of narrators around al-Miqdām, as well as the non-Shāmī corroboration in the paths of Ibn ʿUyaynah. It is unlikely that these are mistakes or forgeries due to the number of solid paths and their independence from one another.

---

196 Al-Sijistānī, *Sunan Abī Dāwūd,* p. 446.
197 Al-ʿAsqalānī, *Tahḏīb al-Tahḏīb*, 1/179.
198 Ibid.
199 Al-Ṭabarānī, *al-Duʿāʾ*, 2/864.

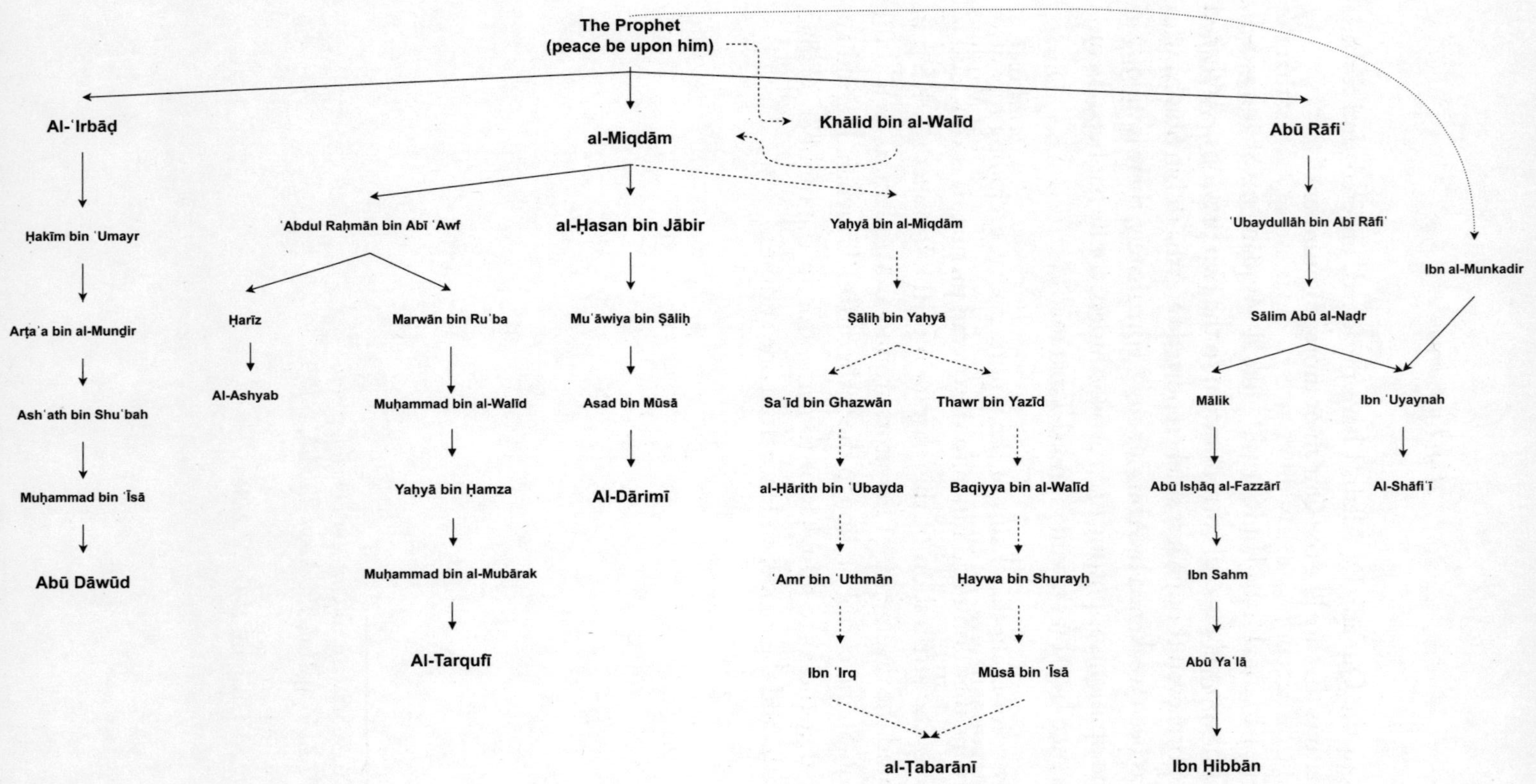
The Prophet
(peace be upon him)
Al-ʿIrbāḍ
al-Miqdām
Khālid bin al-Walīd
Abū Rāfiʿ
Ḥakīm bin ʿUmayr
Arṭaʾa bin al-Munḍir
Ashʿath bin Shuʿbah
Muḥammad bin ʿĪsā
Abū Dāwūd
ʿAbdul Raḥmān bin Abī ʿAwf
Ḥarīz
Al-Ashyab
Marwān bin Ruʿba
Muḥammad bin al-Walīd
Yaḥyā bin Ḥamza
Muḥammad bin al-Mubārak
Al-Tarqufī
al-Ḥasan bin Jābir
Muʿāwiya bin Ṣāliḥ
Asad bin Mūsā
Al-Dārimī
Yaḥyā bin al-Miqdām
Ṣāliḥ bin Yaḥyā
Saʿīd bin Ghazwān
Thawr bin Yazīd
al-Ḥārith bin ʿUbayda
Baqiyya bin al-Walīd
ʿAmr bin ʿUthmān
Ḥaywa bin Shurayḥ
Ibn ʿIrq
Mūsā bin ʿĪsā
al-Ṭabarānī
ʿUbaydullāh bin Abī Rāfiʿ
Ibn al-Munkadir
Sālim Abū al-Naḍr
Mālik
Ibn ʿUyaynah
Abū Isḥāq al-Fazzārī
Al-Shāfiʿī
Ibn Sahm
Abū Yaʿlā
Ibn Ḥibbān

Conclusion

The three reports contain differences in the text that suggest that the narration was reported non-verbatim or that these were statements made on different occasions by the Prophet ﷺ. A student of *ḥadīth* and believer in the system will appreciate the fact that this report was preserved through the centuries, affirming a sign of prophethood. After all, this is a narration about the Prophet ﷺ foreshadowing the emergence of a movement that would come into existence. During his time, the concept of Qur'ān-only didn't exist. His word was final and whatever he said was considered law. The idea that Muslims would actually follow his message but only limit it to the Qur'ān would have been unthinkable to his companions around him. He knew that there will be a group of people that will read Q. 4:59, which orders them to "follow the Messenger," but they simply wouldn't, while simultaneously attempting to follow the rest of the Qur'ān.

A Message to Qur'ānists

Over the past pages, you've come across arguments that demonstrate the unsustainability of the Qur'ān-only method. You're now aware that the Companions did not abide to it nor did a sect of *ḥadīth*-rejecters emerge at their time. You recognize that the Qur'ān didn't simply fall onto your lap from the heavens and that your disconnection from history creates more problems than it solves. You also realize that without knowing the historical context, some of the Qur'ān wouldn't make much sense. However, despite all of this, some of you may still be latching onto the idea that none of this matters and that the Qur'ān orders you to reject everyone and everything outside of it.

This is false. There is not a verse in the Qur'ān that says so. It is your interpretation of the Qur'ān that caused you to arrive at this conclusion; an interpretation that conflicted with the understanding of the Companions of the Prophet ﷺ that willingly narrated his *ḥadīths*.

What should we expect if the Qur'ān-only approach was what Allah had intended?

Firstly, we would find a split among the Companions of the Prophet ﷺ, with a large camp advocating the Qur'ān-only approach. We would find them quoting the verses that Qur'ānists quote in order to support their views. Their statements would have been recorded in the same way that all "problematic" statements have been documented; such is the nature of classical Muslim scholarship.

The earliest polemical works are refutations against the Jahmiyyah sect. Where are the refutations against Qur'ānists? Who are the notable Qur'ānists that advocated for this position? Who is the Jahm bin Ṣafwān of Qur'ānism? What happened to the Wāṣil bin 'Aṭā' of the *ḥadīth*-rejection movement? They simply didn't exist. The Sunnīs documented biographies of the biggest innovators that went against orthodoxy, but there is nothing about Qur'ānists.

More importantly, we would have found every detail to the prayers and the alms within the Qur'ān, instead of leaving them up to the interpretation of Qur'ānists that often conflict with one another. During a live-stream several months ago, the panel that I was on posed the question of "how many times do you pray per day and how many *raka'āt* do you perform in each prayer?" Each of the Qur'ānist participants provided a completely different answer with the utmost conviction.

Did Allah the All-Wise intend for us to have different interpretations for something as simple as the mandatory prayers? If that is the case, then the Qur'ān cannot be considered clear. Anyone claiming that the guesswork involved in extracting the number of prayers in the Qur'ān as "clear" is deluding themselves, for there is no classical scholar that ever extracted these meanings in such a manner.

A Qur'ānist may claim: "It matters not to me if Allah didn't guide them when He guided me!"

By making such a claim, you are missing the point. Your Creator revealed the Qur'ān with the intention to guide, not to create confusion. There is no wisdom in revealing verses ordering a set of actions that will only be understood centuries after the time of revelation.

However, if we look into the first century of Islam, despite the differences among Muslims, political and religious, we find uniformity in the number of prayers and *raka'āt.* This uniformity is not due to them being like-minded in their attempts to tie verses with one another in the same way Qur'ānists do, but it is due to their adherence to the clear *sunnah*, which they learned from the Companions of the Prophet ﷺ, which they in turn learned from him.

بِالْبَيِّنَاتِ وَالزُّبُرِ ۗ وَأَنزَلْنَا إِلَيْكَ الذِّكْرَ لِتُبَيِّنَ لِلنَّاسِ مَا نُزِّلَ إِلَيْهِمْ وَلَعَلَّهُمْ يَتَفَكَّرُونَ ﴿٤٤﴾

> [We sent them] with clear proofs and divine Books. And We have sent down to you [O Prophet] the Reminder, so that you may explain to people what has been revealed for them, and perhaps they will reflect. (Q. 16:44)

May Allah have mercy upon Yaḥyā and Aḥmad and may He reunite them on thrones in paradise.

Works Cited

Aḥmad, ʿAbd al-Razzāq Ḥusayn. *al-Makkī wal-Madanī fī al-Qur'ān al-Karīm*, Cairo: Dār ʿAffān, 1999.

Ahmad, Ṣalāḥ al-Dīn Maqbūl. *Zawābiʿ fī Wajh al-Sunnah*. Kuwait: Dār Ibn al-Athīr, 1994.

Al-Aṣbahānī, Abū Nuʿaym. *al-Mustakhraj ʿalā Ṣaḥīḥ al-Bukhārī*. Algiers: *Dār al-Mīrāth al-Nabawī*, 2019.

Al-Aṣbaḥī, Mālik bin Anas. *al-Mudawwana al-Kubrā*. Beirut: Dār al-Kutub al-ʿIlmiyyāh, 1994.

________. *al-Muwaṭṭá*. Beirut: Dār al-Maʿrifa, 2008.

Al-Ashyab, al-Ḥasan bin Mūsā. *Juz' al-Ḥasan bin Mūsā al-Ashyab*. Fujairah: Dār ʿUlūm al-*Ḥadīth*, 1990.

Al-ʿAsqalānī, Ibn Ḥajar. *al-Maṭālib al-ʿĀliya*. Beirut: Dār al-Kutub al-ʿIlmiyyāh, 2003.

________. *Tahḏīb al-Tahḏīb*. Beirut: Mu'asasat al-Risāla, 2008.

Al-Azharī, Muḥammad bin Aḥmad. *Muʿjam Tahḏīb al-Luġa*. Beirut: Dār al-Maʿrifa, 2001.

Al-Baġdādī, Al-Khaṭīb. *Tārīkh Ba*ġdād. Beirut: Dār al-Kutub al-ʿIlmiyyāh, 2004.

________. *Taqyīd al-ʿIlm*. Beirut: al-Maktaba al-ʿAṣriyya, 2001.

Al-Bukhārī, Muḥammad bin Ismāʿīl. *Ṣaḥīḥ al-Bukhārī*. Riyadh: Darrussalām, 1999.

Al-Dārimī, ʿAbdullāh bin ʿAbdul Raḥmān. *Musnad al-Dārimī*. Beirut: Dār al-Kutub al-ʿIlmiyyāh, 1996.

Al-Fayḍī, Maḥfūẓ al-Raḥmān. *Thunā'iyāt Muwaṭṭà Mālik*. Kuwait: Ġirās, 2012.

Al-Fayrūzābādī, Muḥammad bin Yaʿqūb. *al-Qāmūs al-Muḥīt*. Beirut: Mu'asassat al-Risāla, 2009.

Al-Ḥajūrī, ʿAbdul Karīm bin Aḥmad. *Talbiyat al-Amānī bi-Afrād al-Imām al-Bukhārī*. Sana'a: Makatbat Ṣanʿā' al-Athariyyah, 2004.

Al-Haythamī, ʿAlī bin Sulaymān. *Buġyat al-Bāḥith ʿan Zawā'id Musnad al-Ḥārith*. Madinah: al-Jāmiʿa al-Islāmiyya, 1992.

Al-Jurjānī, ʿAbdullāh bin ʿAdī. *Al-Kāmil fī Ḍuʿafā' al-Rijāl*. Beirut: Dār al-Kutub al-ʿIlmiyyāh, 1997.

Al-Kirmānī, Ḥarb bin Ismāʿīl. *Masā'il Ḥarb bin Ismāʿīl al-Kirmānī*. Riyadh: Dār Ibn al-Athīr, 2010.

Al-Madanī, Ismāʿīl bin Jaʿfar. *Ḥādīth ʿAlī bin Ḥajar al-Saʿdī ʿan Ismāʿīl bin Jaʿfar al-Madanī*. Riyadh: Maktabat al-Rushd, 1998.

Al-Marwazī, Muḥammad bin Naṣr. *Taʿẓīm Qadr al-Ṣalāt*. Mansoura: Dār al-Hadī al-Nabawī, 2011.

Al-Mizzī, Abū al-Ḥajjāj Yūsuf. *Tahḏīb al-Kamāl*. Beirut: Mu'assasat al-Risāla, 1992.

Al-Nasā'ī, Aḥmad bin Shu'ayb. *al-Sunan al-Kubrā*. Riyadh: Maktabat al-Rushd, 2006.

Al-Nīsāpūrī, Muslim bin Ḥajjāj. *Ṣaḥīḥ Muslim*. Beirut: Dār al-Ma'rifa, 2007.

Al-Qaysī, Makkī bin Abī Ṭālib. *al-Ibāna 'an Ma'ānī al-Qirā'āt*. Beirut: Books – Publisher, 2011.

Al-Ṣan'ānī, Abd al-Razzāq bin Hammām. *Al-Muṣannaf*. Beirut: Dār Iḥyā' al-Turāth, 2002.

________. *Tafsīr Abd al-Razzāq*. Dār al-Kutub al-'Ilmiyyāh, 1999.

Al-Shāfi'ī, Muḥammad bin Idrīs. *al-Umm*. Beirut: Dār Ibn Ḥazm, 2005.

Al-Sijistānī, Abū Bakr bin Abī Dāwūd. *Al-Ma ṣāḥif*. Beirut: Dār al-Bashā'ir, 2002.

Al-Sijistānī, Muḥammad bin 'Uzayz. *Nuzhat al-Qulūb fī Tafsīr Ġarīb al-Qur'ān al-'Azīz*. Beirut: Dār al-Ma'rifa, 2010.

Al-Sijistānī, Sulaymān bin Al-Ash'ath. *Risālat Abī Dāwūd ilā Ahl Makkah*. Beirut: al-Maktab al-Islāmī, 1984.

________. *Sunan Abī Dāwūd*. Riyadh: Dārrussalām, 1999.

Al-Suyūṭī, Jalāluddīn. *al-Itqān fī 'Ulūm al-Qur'ān*. Beirut: Mu'asasat al-Risāla, 2008.

Al-Suyūṭī, Jalāluddīn. *Qaṭf al-Azhār al-Mutanāthira fī al-Akhbār al-Mutawātira*. Beirut: Al-Maktab al-Islāmī, 1985.

Al-Ṭabarānī, Sulaymān bin Aḥmad. *al-Du'ā'*. Beirut: Dār al-Bashā'ir, 1987.

________. *al-Mu'jam al-Kabīr*. Beirut: Mu'assasat al-Rayyān, 2010.

Al-Ṭabarī, Muḥammad bin Jarīr. *Tafsīr al-Ṭabarī*. Dār al-Kutub al-'Ilmiyyāh, 1992.

________. *Tahḏīb al-Āthār (al-Juz' al-Mafqūd)*. Damascus: Dār al-Ma̓mūn lil-Turāth, 1995.

Al-Tarqufī, 'Abbās bin 'Abdillāh. *Juz' al-Tarqufī*. Sharjah: Maktabat al-Ṣaḥāba, 2009.

Al-Ṭayālisī, Abū Dāwūd Sulaymān bin Dāwūd, *Musnad Abī Dāwūd Al-Ṭayālisī*, Beirut: Dār Ibn Ḥazm, 2013.

Al-Tirmiḏī, Muḥammad bin 'Īsā. *Al-Jāmi'al-Kabīr*. Al-Jubail: Dār al-Siddīq, 2012.

Al-Yaḥṣubī, Al-Qāḍī 'Iyāḍ. *Tartīb al-Madārik*. Beirut: Mu'asasat al-Risāla, 2014.

Azami, Muḥammad Muṣṭafā. *Dirāsāt fī al-Ḥadīth al-Nabawī*. Beirut: al-Maktab al-Islāmī, 1992.

Ibn 'Abd al-Barr, Yūsuf bin 'Abdillāh. *al-Tamhīd*. Beirut: Dār al-Fikr,2005.

Ibn Abī Shayba, Abū Bakr. *al-Muṣannaf*. Beirut: Dār al-Kutub al-'Ilmiyyāh, 1995.

Ibn al-Ja'd, 'Alī. *Musnad Ibn al-Ja'd*, Beirut: Dār al-Kutub al-'Ilmiyyāh, 1996.

Ibn al-Jazarī, Abū al-Khayr Muḥammad. *Ġayat al-Nihāya fī Ṭabaqāt al-Qurrā'*. Beirut: Dār al-Kutub al-ʿIlmiyyāh, 2006.

Ibn Khuzayma. Muḥammad bin Isḥāq. *Ṣaḥīḥ Ibn Khuzayma*. Beirut: al-Maktab al-Islāmī, 2003.

Ibn Ḥanbal, Aḥmad bin Muḥammad. *Musnad Aḥmad.* Riyadh: Dārrussalām, 2013.

Ibn Ḥazm, ʿAlī bin Aḥmad. *Asmā' al-Ṣaḥāba al-Ruwāt.* Beirut: Dār al-Kutub al-ʿIlmiyyāh, 1992.

________. *Al-Muḥallā.* Amman: Bayt al-Afkār al-Duwaliyya.

Ibn Ḥibbān, Abū Ḥātim Muḥammad. *al-Iḥsān fī Taqrīb Ṣaḥīḥ Ibn Ḥibbān*, Beirut: Dār al-Maʿrifa, 2004.

Ibn al-Mundir, Muḥammad bin Ibrāhīm. *al-Ijmāʿ.* Cairo: Maktabat Awlād al-Shaykh, 2011.

________. *al-Awsaṭ min al-Sunan wal-Ijmāʿ wal-Ikhtilāf.* Faiyum: Dār al-Falāḥ, 2015.

Ibn Saʿd, Muḥammad. *al-Ṭabaqāt al-Kabīr.* Cairo: al-Khānjī, 2012.

Ibn Sallām, Abū ʿUbayd al-Qāsim. *Faḍā'il al-Qur'ān.* Beirut: Dār al-Kutub al-ʿIlmiyyāh, 1991.

Ibn Shabba, Abū Zayd ʿUmar. *Tārīkh al-Madīna.* Beirut: Dār al-Kutub al-ʿIlmiyyāh, 1996.

Lane, Edward William. *An Arabic–English Lexicon.* London: Williams and Norgate, 1863.

Sanjar, Abū Saʿīd. *Musnad al-Shāfiʿī*. Kuwait: Ġirās, 2004.